PASTA
AND
PIZZAS

MARGARET FULTON'S BOOK OF PASTA AND PIZZAS

octopus

CONTENTS

This edition published 1992 by
Reed Consumer Books
Michelin House
81 Fulham Road
London SW3 6RB

ISBN 0 7064 4011 0

Printed in China

INTRODUCTION

Pasta and pizzas are now part of international cuisine.

Pasta is served at least once every day in most Italian homes. It is to the Italians what potatoes are to the English.

Pasta is very satisfying to make, it does take a little time and patience but is well worth the trouble and there are excellent pasta machines on the market to help. Commercial pasta comes in all shapes and sizes and there are many fresh pasta shops opening throughout Australia.

You will find pizza huts as far away as London to Los Angeles, Tokyo to Tallahassee, and they are made in homes throughout the world. You can make them or buy them made with a countless variety of fillings. A good pizza is a beautiful thing to look at with its crisp, golden crust, containing a wonderful fresh tomato sauce, black olives, salami, melting mozzarella and a sprinkling of herbs.

Washed down with a goodly quantity of light wine, pasta and pizzas each make a delicious and substantial meal. These recipes will remind you of the good life, as lived in Italy. Enjoy cooking, serving and eating them!

Margaret Fulton

NOTES

Standard spoon measurements are used in all recipes.
1 tablespoon = one 20 ml spoon
1 teaspoon = one 5 ml spoon
All spoon measures are level.
Standard cup = 250 ml

Fresh herbs are used unless otherwise stated. If unobtainable substitute a bouquet garni of the equivalent dried herbs, or use dried herbs instead but halve the quantities stated.

Use freshly ground black pepper where pepper is specified.

If fresh yeast is unobtainable, substitute dried yeast but use only half the stated quantity and follow the manufacturer's instructions for reconstituting.

Ovens should be preheated to the specified temperature.

For all recipes, quantities are given in both metric and imperial measures. Follow either set but not a mixture of both, because they are not interchangeable.

Recipes for basic pasta and pizza doughs are given in the introductory copy. Detailed instructions for cooking pasta are given in the introduction. Refer to these where the copy is marked with an asterisk.

PASTA

Pasta is one of the easiest dishes in the world to prepare. It is also one of the easiest to ruin. More often than not, it is ruined by not following a few essential cooking rules.

Pasta is a good source of protein and the wholewheat variety has a high fibre content. If you are counting calories, reduce the amount of butter and oil used in the recipes and choose a sauce which is low in calories.

As well as the many dried varieties of pasta available, an increasing number of stores now sell fresh pasta. This is, by far, preferable to the dried type as it is very near the flavour and texture of homemade pasta.

Anyone who is adept at pastry-making will have no trouble in making their own pasta. It may take a few practice runs, but it is well worth the trouble. Don't give up after the first attempt – practice really does make perfect. Homemade pasta has an individual flavour which will certainly be appreciated.

Most of the recipes in this book use fresh pasta, which can be the bought variety or your own homemade if time allows. Allow about 125 g (4 oz) fresh pasta per person for a main course, depending on how substantial the sauce is and the size of the appetite, and about 60 g (2 oz) for a starter. If dried pasta is used, it is specified in the recipe. If you choose to use a dried variety instead of fresh, allow 60-90 g (2-3 oz) dried pasta per person for a main course, and 30-60 g (1-2 oz) for a starter.

The pasta dough on page 10 can be used to make all types of pasta. It is referred to in the recipes as '500 g (1 lb) quantity pasta dough', where it is intended homemade dough should be used, although you may buy it ready-made in the piece if preferred. If you use the dough recipe to make your own tagliatelle, etc, either adjust the basic recipe to give you the amount specified, or make it all up and keep any leftover pasta dough in the freezer for up to 3 months.

Cooking Pasta

All pasta must be cooked in plenty of water. As a guide, allow at least 4 litres (16 cups) water for 500 g (1 lb) pasta. Never use less than 3 litres (12 cups) even for a small amount. Do not attempt to cook more than 1 kg (2 lb) in one pan, as it is difficult to stir, season and drain. The addition of oil prevents the pasta pieces from sticking together.

Bring the water, 1-2 tablespoons oil and 1-2 tablespoons salt to the boil. Add the pasta, return to the boil and ensure that the pasta is well covered with water.

Cook uncovered, stirring occasionally, until *al dente* – just tender but firm to the bite. For fresh pasta this will take about 2 to 3 minutes (5 to 10 minutes for filled types); dried pasta will take about 9 to 12 minutes. Do *not* simply follow the

manufacturer's cooking times or the recipe – test the pasta frequently during cooking. Pasta that is overcooked and soft is unappetizing.

As soon as it is *al dente*, drain the pasta to stop it softening further, toss in butter and coat in sauce to prevent it drying out. Serve immediately, accompanied by freshly grated Parmesan.

Types of Pasta

The varieties of pasta are endless. Freshly made tagliatelle, fettuccine and spaghetti are available in good supermarkets and delicatessens, as well as some stuffed varieties such as tortellini and ravioli.

There is an excellent range of dried pasta in most stores. A selection of the many varieties available is illustrated overleaf. For those of us in a hurry, there is an excellent dried lasagne on the market which requires no pre-cooking, so it can be used in the same way as freshly made lasagne. Follow the manufacturer's instructions for its use.

DRIED PASTA VARIETIES

1. Pasta twists
2. Tortellini
3. Pasta bow ties
4. Pasta shells
5. Wholewheat macaroni
6. Pasta whirls
7. Pasta spirals
8. Tagliatelle verdi
9. Tagliatelle
10. Wholewheat tagliatelle

11. Rigatoni
12. Small pasta shells
13. Wholewheat spaghetti
14. Pasta wheels
15. Spaghetti
16. Vermicelli
17. Lasagne verdi
18. Lasagne
19. Wholewheat rigatoni
20. Pasta quills

EGG PASTA DOUGH

4 cups plain flour
good pinch of salt
2 large or 3 medium eggs
1 teaspoon oil
3-4 tablespoons water

Sift the flour and salt into a large bowl. Make a hollow in the centre and drop in the eggs and oil. Draw the flour into the centre, beating, add 3 tablespoons water and knead well; add another tablespoon of water if the mixture is too dry.

Knead the dough until smooth and very elastic; this is essential, or the dough will not roll properly. Wrap the dough in clingfilm and leave to rest for a minimum of 15 minutes and a maximum of 2 hours.

Makes a 500 g (1 lb) quantity

NOTE: For wholemeal pasta, use 4 cups wholemeal flour, 3 large eggs and about 4-5 tablespoons water.

SPINACH AND EGG PASTA DOUGH

350 g (12 oz) plain flour
good pinch of salt
125 g (4 oz) cooked leaf spinach, well drained and finely chopped
2 large or 3 medium eggs
1 teaspoon oil

Follow the directions for the basic egg pasta dough (above), adding the spinach with the eggs.

Makes a 500 g (1 lb) quantity

NOTE: This pasta is easier to make than the egg pasta. It is easier to work as it does not dry out as quickly.

To Roll Out Pasta Dough

Roll out the dough on a lightly floured board or in a pasta machine. Rolling by hand is preferable, but a pasta machine makes the job a lot easier and quicker. If using a machine, follow the manufacturer's instructions.

The rolling process is very important and it is well worth taking the time to achieve a good result. Do not give up if the first result is inedible and disappointing – practice certainly does make perfect in this instance.

Flatten the dough with the rolling pin, giving the dough a quarter turn between each roll, until it measures 20-23 cm (8-9 inches) in diameter.

Hold the near edge of the dough down with one hand and place the rolling pin on the opposite edge. Push the rolling pin as follows to stretch the dough; *do not roll.* Curl the end of the dough around the pin and push with the pin to stretch the dough. Keep moving the pin towards you along the dough, stopping, stretching the dough, then rolling up more dough, until you have taken up all the dough. Give the pin a quarter turn so that it points towards you and unfurl the sheet of dough, opening it up flat.

Repeat the rolling and stretching until the dough is once again completely wrapped around the pin. Turn the pin round again, unwrap the dough and repeat the procedure. Continue until a 500 g (1 lb) quantity pasta dough has been stretched to a square measuring about 40-45 cm (16-18 inches). This process must be done very quickly to prevent the dough drying out; if this happens, it will be ruined.

Roll out the dough until it is paper thin, then use as required.

PIZZAS

There are three ways of making basic pizza doughs. The one I recommend is the traditional bread dough, which is made with strong flour and yeast. This is the one specified for all the recipes in this book.

If time is short, a packet of commercially made bread mix can be used instead. It is equally good and has the advantage of being quick and very easy. Follow the packet instructions exactly, then roll out evenly and use as indicated in each recipe.

Ready-made pizza bases and jars of pizza sauce are available from many supermarkets – a definite boon when you need an instant snack.

As a last resort, a scone dough can be used – but please don't expect the same results. It is a substitute though it does not give a real Italian texture or flavour.

PIZZA DOUGH

1½ cups plain flour
1 teaspoon salt
1 tablespoon olive oil
15 g (1½ oz) fresh yeast, crumbled or 1 packet dried yeast
½ cup lukewarm water

Sift the flour and salt into a large bowl. Add the oil and yeast to the water and add to well in flour. Knead to a soft, elastic dough; this will take about 8 minutes by hand or 4 to 5 minutes in a food processor or electric blender. Cover and leave to rise in a warm place for 2 hours, until doubled in size.

Makes one 25 cm (10 inch) pizza

To Roll Out Pizza Dough

Place the dough on a floured board and knead lightly. Roll out to a 25-30 cm (10-12 inch) circle, about 5 mm (¼ inch) thick, turning the dough as it is rolled to prevent shrinking. Using the fingertips, push some of the dough from the centre towards the edge, making the edge about twice as thick as the rest of the circle.

Place the dough on a lightly floured baking tray proceed as directed in each recipe.

If the recipe states 'place the pizza on a hot baking sheet', put the baking sheet in the oven to warm while preheating the oven. Leave it in there until it is really hot. This is most important, as it ensures that the pizza will have a crisp base and that the top and base will cook evenly.

PASTA STARTERS

TAGLIATELLE WITH ASPARAGUS

90 g (3 oz) butter
2 cloves garlic, crushed
500 g (1 lb) thin asparagus spears, cut into 2.5 cm (1 inch) lengths
1¼ cups cream
1 tablespoon each chopped parsley and thyme
salt and pepper
500 g (1 lb) fresh tagliatelle
½ cup parmesan cheese, grated
thyme or parsley sprigs to garnish

Heat 60 g (2 oz) of the butter in a wok or frying pan, add the garlic and asparagus and cook gently, without browning, for 7 to 10 minutes, until the asparagus is just tender. Add the cream, herbs, and salt and pepper to taste. Remove from the heat.

Cook the pasta until *al dente**. Drain thoroughly and turn into a warmed serving dish. Add the remaining butter and toss well.

Return the sauce to the heat for 1 minute, then pour over the pasta. Sprinkle with the parmesan cheese and garnish with thyme or parsley sprigs. Serve immediately.

Serves 6

FETTUCCINE WITH ZUCCHINI

750 g (1½ lb) small zucchini
salt
½ cup plain flour
oil for shallow frying
4 cloves garlic
500 g (1 lb) fresh fettuccine or fine noodles
60 g (2 oz) butter
12 basil leaves, torn into 2 or 3 pieces
½ cup parmesan cheese, grated
basil sprigs to garnish

Cut the zucchini into 5 cm (2 inch) lengths and arrange in layers in a colander, sprinkling each layer liberally with salt. Leave to drain for 1 to 2 hours. Rinse well and dry thoroughly on kitchen paper. Toss in the flour.

Heat the oil in a frying pan, add the whole garlic cloves and fry until coloured, then remove. Add the zucchini in batches and fry until golden. Drain on kitchen paper and keep hot.

Meanwhile, cook the pasta until *al dente**. Drain and turn into a warmed serving dish. Add the butter and basil and toss well. Stir in the zucchini, sprinkle with the cheese and garnish with basil. Serve immediately.

Serves 6

MEAT-STUFFED CANNELLONI

1 tablespoon oil
1 large onion, chopped
1 clove garlic, crushed
185 g (6 oz) minced beef
60 g (2 oz) mortadella, chopped
½ teaspoon dried mixed herbs
pinch of grated nutmeg
salt and pepper
1 egg yolk
250 g (8 oz) ricotta or curd cheese
1 cup grated parmesan cheese
*250 g (8 oz) quantity pasta dough**

MEAT SAUCE:
1 tablespoon oil
1 onion, chopped
1 clove garlic, crushed
185 g (6 oz) minced beef
6 tomatoes
1 tablespoon each chopped basil and marjoram
⅔ cup dry white wine

TOPPING:
185 g (6 oz) mozzarella cheese, sliced
2 tablespoons grated parmesan cheese
2 tablespoons dried breadcrumbs

Heat the oil in a pan, add the onion and garlic and cook for 2 minutes, without browning. Increase the heat, add the beef and brown quickly.

Add the mortadella, herbs, nutmeg, and salt and pepper to taste. Cook, uncovered, for 15 minutes, stirring occasionally. Remove from the heat, stir in the egg yolk and cheeses and mix well. Set aside to cool.

To make the meat sauce, heat the oil in a pan, add the onion and garlic and cook for 2 minutes, without browning. Increase the heat, add the beef and brown quickly.

Skin, seed and chop the tomatoes, and add to the pan with the herbs, and salt and pepper to taste. Pour over the wine, bring to the boil and cook rapidly for 15 to 20 minutes, until reduced and thickened. Set aside.

Cut the pasta dough into 7 × 10 cm (3 × 4 inch) sheets and cook until just *al dente**. Drain thoroughly and lay on clean dry tea-towels.

Divide the stuffing between the pasta sheets and roll up from the shorter side. Arrange in a single layer, seam side down, in a lightly greased ovenproof dish. Spoon over the sauce.

Place the mozzarella cheese slices on top and sprinkle with the parmesan and breadcrumbs. Bake in a preheated hot oven, 200°C (400°F), for 15 to 20 minutes, until golden brown. Serve immediately.

Serves 6 to 8

NOTE: This may also be served as a main course for 4 people.

SPAGHETTI WITH TOMATO AND CHEESE SAUCE

1 kg (2 lb) tomatoes
1 celery stick
1 carrot, chopped
2 onions, chopped
⅔ cup dry white wine
2 tablespoons chopped marjoram
30 g (1 oz) matured cheddar cheese, grated
2 tablespoons grated parmesan cheese
salt and pepper
500 g (1 lb) fresh spaghetti
30 g (1 oz) butter

Roughly chop the tomatoes and celery and place in a pan with the carrot and onions. Bring slowly to the boil, cover and simmer for 30 minutes. Rub through a sieve and return to the pan.

Add the wine, bring to the boil and cook for 15 to 20 minutes, until the sauce has reduced and thickened. Remove from the heat and stir in the marjoram, cheeses, and salt and pepper to taste.

Cook the spaghetti until *al dente**. Drain thoroughly and turn into a warmed serving dish. Add the butter and toss well. Heat the sauce thoroughly and pour over the pasta. Serve immediately.

Serves 6

NOODLES WITH SWEET PEPPER SAUCE

2 red peppers
250 g (8 oz) tomatoes
2 tablespoons oil
1 onion, chopped
salt and pepper
250 g (8 oz) Italian salami, chopped
250 g (8 oz) fresh egg tagliatelle
250 g (8 oz) fresh tagliatelle verdi
30 g (1 oz) butter
¼ cup (1 oz) grated parmesan cheese (optional)
TO GARNISH:
red pepper slices
thyme sprigs

Remove the core and seeds from the peppers. Peel thinly and cut into 1 cm (½ inch) squares. Skin, seed and chop the tomatoes.

Heat the oil in a pan, add the onion and cook for 5 minutes, until golden brown, stirring. Lower heat, add the peppers and cook for 7 to 8 minutes, until soft, stirring occasionally.

Add the tomatoes and cook for 3 minutes. Season liberally with salt and pepper. Add the salami, check the seasoning and remove from the heat.

Meanwhile, cook the pasta until *al dente**. Drain thoroughly and turn into a warmed serving dish. Add the butter and toss well.

Return the sauce to the heat and boil for 1 minute. Pour over the pasta, sprinkle with the parmesan cheese, if using, and garnish with pepper slices and thyme. Serve immediately.

Serves 6

CRESCIONI

*500 g (1 lb) quantity pasta dough**
750 g (1½ lb) spinach
30 g (1 oz) butter
1-2 cloves garlic, crushed
90 g (3 oz) Boursin cheese with garlic
pinch of grated nutmeg
1 tablespoon each chopped chives, parsley and marjoram
salt and pepper
a little beaten egg
oil for shallow frying
3-4 tablespoons grated parmesan cheese

Roll out the pasta dough very thinly, cover with plastic wrap and leave to rest for 5 minutes.

Cook the spinach, with just the water clinging to the leaves after washing, for 3 minutes. Drain well and chop roughly.

Melt the butter in a frying pan, add the garlic and cook for 2 minutes, without browning. Stir in the spinach, cheese, nutmeg, herbs, salt to taste and lots of pepper.

Cut the pasta into 7 cm (3 inch) squares. Place a teaspoon of the filling in the centre of each square, brush the edges with beaten egg, fold over like a turnover and seal firmly. Place on a tea-towel to dry for 1 hour. Heat the oil in a frying pan, add a few crescioni at a time and fry for 3 minutes each side, until golden. Drain on kitchen paper and place in a warmed dish.

Sprinkle with the parmesan cheese and serve immediately.

Serves 6

TAGLIATELLE WITH FOUR CHEESES

60 g (2 oz) butter
1 onion, chopped
2-3 cloves garlic, crushed
125 g (4 oz) streaky bacon, derinded and diced
90 g (3 oz) each Bel Paese, matured cheddar and gruyère cheese, grated
½ cup grated parmesan cheese
1¼ cups cream
500 g (1 lb) fresh wholewheat tagliatelle
2 tablespoons each chopped parsley and chives
1 tablespoon chopped basil

Melt half the butter in a saucepan, add the onion and garlic and cook, without browning, for 2 to 3 minutes. Add the bacon and cook for 5 minutes, stirring occasionally. Stir in the cheeses and cream. Remove from the heat.

Cook the pasta until *al dente**. Drain thoroughly and turn into a warmed serving dish. Add the remaining butter and toss well.

Return the sauce to the heat and stir in the herbs. Pour over the pasta and mix well. Serve immediately.

Serves 4 to 6

SPAGHETTI WITH GARLIC AND OIL

500 g (1 lb) fresh spaghetti
10 tablespoons olive oil
4 cloves garlic, crushed
30 g (1 oz) butter
3 tablespoons chopped parsley

Cook the spaghetti until *al dente**.

Meanwhile, heat the oil in a pan, add the garlic and fry until golden, stirring constantly.

Drain the spaghetti and turn into a warmed serving dish. Add the butter and toss well. Pour over the oil and garlic and mix well. Stir in the parsley and serve immediately.

Serves 6

RAVIOLI ALLA FIORENTINA

1 kg (2 lb) spinach
125 g (4 oz) butter
1/4 cup plain flour
250 g (8 oz) ricotta or curd cheese
3 egg yolks
pinch of grated nutmeg
salt and pepper
1/2 cup grated parmesan cheese
lime or lemon slices to garnish (optional)

Cook the spinach, with just the water clinging to its leaves after washing, for 3 minutes. Drain and cool under cold running water. Drain thoroughly and press well with the hands to remove all the moisture. Chop finely and set aside.

Melt 30 g (1 oz) of the butter in a pan, stir in the flour and cook for 2 minutes, stirring. Add the ricotta or curd cheese.

Lower the heat and add the spinach, egg yolks, nutmeg, and salt and pepper to taste. Cook, stirring constantly, for 1 minute, taking care not to curdle the egg. Remove from the heat and leave until completely cold.

Roll into pointed sausage shapes about 2.5 cm (1 inch) in length and place on a board to dry for 1 hour.

Cook in batches, in boiling salted water, for about 4 minutes; they are cooked when they rise to the surface. Remove with a slotted spoon and place in a warmed serving dish.

Add the remaining butter and toss well. Sprinkle with the parmesan. Garnish with lime or lemon slices if liked, and serve immediately.

Serves 6

NOODLES WITH FISH SAUCE

10 anchovies
2-3 tablespoons milk
90 g (3 oz) butter
1 large onion, chopped
1-2 cloves garlic, very thinly sliced
⅔ cup dry white wine
1 cup fish stock (see below)
185 g (6 oz) peeled prawns
salt and pepper
2-3 tablespoons chopped parsley
500 g (1 lb) fresh noodles
TO GARNISH:
anchovy fillets
whole prawns

Soak the anchovies in the milk for 30 minutes, drain, chop and set aside.

Melt 60 g (2 oz) of the butter in a pan, add the onion and cook until golden brown. Add the garlic and cook for 1 minute. Add the wine, bring to the boil and cook rapidly until reduced by half. Add the fish stock, anchovies, prawns, and salt and pepper to taste and cook, uncovered, for 2 minutes. Remove from the heat and stir in the parsley.

Cook the noodles until *al dente**. Drain thoroughly and turn into a warmed serving dish. Add the remaining butter and toss well.

Heat the sauce for 1 minute, pour over the noodles and toss well. Garnish with a lattice of anchovy fillets and whole prawns. Serve immediately with parmesan cheese.

Serves 6

NOTE: To make fish stock, place fish heads and bones in a large pan with 1 onion, 1 carrot and a bouquet garni. Cover with cold water, bring to the boil, then simmer for 1 hour; strain.

RAVIOLI WITH CHICKEN

125 g (4 oz) butter
1 small onion, chopped
60 g (2 oz) button mushrooms, diced
750 g (1½ lb) cooked chicken, minced
½ cup dry white wine
½ cup cream
1 tablespoon chopped parsley
salt and pepper
*500 g (1 lb) quantity pasta dough**
1 beaten egg
4-6 tablespoons grated parmesan cheese
parsley sprigs to garnish

Melt half of the butter in a pan, add the onion and cook for 5 minutes, without browning. Add mushrooms and cook for 2 minutes. Remove from the heat and stir in the chicken, wine, cream, parsley, and salt and pepper to taste. Leave until cold.

Cut the pasta in half. Cover with plastic wrap and rest for 30 minutes.

Place teaspoons of the chicken mixture about 5 cm (2 inches) apart on one piece of pasta. Brush lightly with beaten egg between the filling.

Lay the second sheet of pasta lightly on top, pressing down between the filling to seal. Cut around the filling with a pastry wheel or knife to give little ravioli squares. Check that each ravioli is thoroughly sealed and place on a board to dry for 1 hour.

Cook until *al dente**. Transfer to a warmed serving dish with a slotted spoon. Add the remaining butter and toss well. Sprinkle with parmesan cheese to taste and garnish with parsley. Serve immediately.

Serves 6

SEAFOOD CANNELLONI

2 celery sticks, chopped
2 carrots, chopped
2½ cups milk
1 onion, quartered
3 peppercorns
1 bay leaf
60 g (2 oz) butter
½ cup plain flour
1 tablespoon chopped dill
2 tablespoons chopped parsley
salt and pepper
*250 g (8 oz) quantity pasta dough**
1 tablespoon oil
2 tablespoons dried breadcrumbs

FILLING:
⅔ cup dry white wine
125 g (4 oz) scallops, halved
15 g (½ oz) butter
2 spring onions, chopped
250 g (8 oz) peeled prawns
1 cup grated matured cheddar cheese
4 tablespoons grated parmesan cheese

TO GARNISH:
whole prawns
dill sprigs

Put the celery and carrots in a pan with the milk, onion, peppercorns and bay leaf. Bring to the boil, remove from the heat and leave until cold. Strain and set aside the milk.

Melt the butter in a pan, stir in the flour and cook for 2 minutes, stirring. Gradually add the milk, stirring constantly. Bring to the boil and cook for 2 minutes, stirring. Stir in the herbs and salt to taste.

To make the filling, place the wine in a small pan and bring to the boil. Add the scallops and cook, uncovered, for about 2 minutes, until tender. Remove with a slotted spoon and set aside. Reserve the wine.

Melt the butter in a pan, add the spring onions and cook, without browning, for 1 minute. Add the reserved wine and boil for 1 to 2 minutes until reduced to about 2 tablespoons. Remove from the heat, stir in just over a quarter of the sauce and mix well. Add the prawns, scallops, and salt and pepper to taste. Stir in the cheeses, heating if necessary to melt.

Cut the pasta dough into 7 × 10 cm (3 × 4 inch) sheets and cook in boiling salted water, with the oil added, for 1 minute. Drain thoroughly and lay on clean dry tea-towels.

Divide the filling between the pasta sheets and roll up from the shorter side. Arrange in a single layer, seam side down, in a lightly greased ovenproof dish. Spoon over the sauce and sprinkle with the breadcrumbs.

Cook in a preheated hot oven, 200°C (400°F), for 15 to 20 minutes, until golden. Garnish with prawns and dill and serve immediately.

Serves 6 to 8

NOTE: This may also be served as a main course for 4 people.

NOODLES WITH PISTOU

4 cloves garlic
about 35 basil leaves
about 25 marjoram leaves
50 g (2 oz) butter
1¼ cups cream
salt and pepper
500 g (1 lb) fresh noodles
150 g (5 oz) parmesan cheese, grated
basil or marjoram sprigs to garnish

Crush the garlic and finely chop the herbs. Mix together well. Melt half the butter in a pan and add the herbs. Remove from the heat, stir in the cream, and season well with salt and pepper.

Cook the noodles until *al dente**. Drain well and turn into a warmed serving dish. Add the remaining butter and toss well.

Return the sauce to the heat and stir in the cheese until melted. Pour over the noodles and toss well. Garnish with basil or marjoram and serve immediately.

Serves 6

SMOKED SALMON AND DILL PIZZA

*1 quantity pizza dough**
3 large ripe tomatoes, skinned and sliced
185 g (6 oz) smoked salmon, thinly sliced
1 tablespoon each chopped dill and parsley
125 g (4 oz) mozzarella cheese, sliced

Roll out the dough*. Arrange the tomatoes on the base and lay the salmon on top. Sprinkle with the herbs and cover with the cheese.

Slide the pizza onto a hot baking sheet* and bake at once in a preheated hot oven, 220°C (425°F), for 15 to 20 minutes, until golden. Serve immediately.

Serves 4

NOTE: For a less expensive variation, use peeled prawns instead of salmon.

ROMAN PIZZA

*1 quantity pizza dough**
4 large ripe tomatoes, skinned and sliced
6 basil leaves, finely chopped
1 tablespoon chopped oregano
salt and pepper
125 g (4 oz) ham or prosciutto crudo, thinly sliced
60 g (2 oz) button mushrooms
¾ cup grated matured cheddar cheese

Roll out the dough*. Arrange the tomatoes on the base, sprinkle with the herbs, and season with salt and pepper to taste. Lay the ham on top and sprinkle with the mushrooms and cheese.

Slide the pizza onto a hot baking sheet* and bake at once in a preheated hot oven, 220°C (425°F), until golden. Serve immediately.

Serves 4

TOMATO AND MOZZARELLA PIZZA

500 g (1 lb) ripe plum tomatoes, or 1 × 425 g can tomatoes
2 tablespoons olive oil
1 teaspoon salt
*1 quantity pizza dough**
185 g (6 oz) mozzarella cheese, grated
1 teaspoon dried oregano
1 tablespoon grated parmesan cheese

Roughly chop the tomatoes and place, with their juice, in a frying pan. Add the oil and salt, bring to the boil, cover and cook for 2 minutes. Remove the lid and simmer for 15 minutes, stirring occasionally, until thickened.

Turn the mixture into a sieve and discard any liquid that drains through. Rub the tomatoes through the sieve and leave to cool.

Roll out the dough*. Sprinkle with the mozzarella cheese, spoon over the tomato sauce, then sprinkle with the oregano and parmesan.

Slide the pizza onto a hot baking sheet* and bake in a preheated very hot oven, 230°C (450°F), for 15 to 20 minutes, until golden brown. Serve immediately.

Serves 4

PIZZA PAYSANNE

60 g (2 oz) butter
1 large onion, finely chopped
4 rashers streaky bacon, derinded and chopped
2 potatoes, diced
2 eggs
⅔ cup cream
1 tablespoon each chopped parsley, thyme and chives
salt and pepper
*1 quantity pizza dough**
1 small red pepper, cored, seeded and chopped
1 cup grated matured cheddar cheese

Melt the butter in a pan, add the onion and bacon and cook for about 5 minutes, until lightly browned. Drain on kitchen paper.

Add the potato to the pan and cook, stirring occasionally, until browned. Drain on kitchen paper.

Beat the eggs and cream together. Stir in the herbs and season liberally with salt and pepper.

When the dough has doubled in size*, place it on a floured board and knead thoroughly. Roll out and use to line a 23 cm (9 inch) flan ring placed on a baking sheet.

Spoon the onion, bacon and potato into the case and sprinkle with the red pepper. Pour over the egg mixture and sprinkle with the cheese.

Bake in a preheated hot oven, 200°C (400°F), for 20 to 25 minutes, until well risen and golden. Serve hot or cold.

Serves 4

'TURNED-OVER' PIZZAS

*½ quantity pizza dough**
oil for frying
1 quantity Tomato Sauce (see American Hot Pizza, below)
125 g (4 oz) matured cheddar cheese, diced
2 tablespoons grated parmesan cheese
125 g (4 oz) Italian salami, sliced
1 tablespoon each chopped oregano and basil
1-2 cloves garlic, crushed

When the pizza dough has risen*, divide it into 8 equal pieces and form each into a round.

Heat a little oil in a large heavy-based frying pan and fry 2 rounds at a time for about 2 to 3 minutes on each side, until golden.

Spread the hot Tomato Sauce on the pizzas, and top with the cheeses, salami, herbs and garlic. Return to the pan and cook at a lower heat for 3 minutes. Fold in half and serve immediately.

Serves 4

AMERICAN HOT PIZZA

30 g (1 oz) butter
2 onions, sliced
*1 quantity pizza dough**
2-3 green chillies, seeded and sliced lengthwise
1 tablespoon each chopped thyme and marjoram
30 g (1 oz) each Bel Paese and mozzarella cheese, diced
TOMATO SAUCE:
1-2 tablespoons oil
1 clove garlic, crushed
2-3 shallots, chopped
250 g (8 oz) tomatoes, skinned, seeded and chopped
⅔ cup dry white wine
1 teaspoon dried mixed herbs
salt and pepper
TO GARNISH: *(optional)*:
marjoram sprigs

First make the tomato sauce. Heat the oil in a pan, add the garlic and shallots and cook for about 5 minutes, until golden. Add the tomatoes, wine and mixed herbs. Bring to the boil and cook rapidly for 20 minutes, until thickened. Season with salt and pepper to taste and leave to cool.

Melt the butter in a pan, add the onions and cook for 5 minutes until golden. Leave to cool.

Roll out the dough* and slide the pizza onto a hot baking sheet*. Spread the onions on the base and cover with the tomato sauce. Sprinkle with the chillies, thyme, marjoram and cheeses.

Bake at once in a preheated hot oven, 220°C (425°F), for 15 to 20 minutes, until the dough and topping are golden. Garnish with marjoram if liked, and serve immediately.

Serves 4

SEAFOOD PIZZA

*1 quantity pizza dough**
1 quantity Tomato Sauce (see American Hot Pizza, opposite)
2 tomatoes, skinned and sliced
1 × 200 g can tuna fish
125 g (4 oz) peeled prawns
squeeze of lemon juice
2 teaspoons chopped basil
30 g (1 oz) each matured cheddar and Bel Paese cheese, diced

Roll out the dough* and slide onto a hot baking sheet*. Cover with the Tomato Sauce and place the tomatoes around the edge. Drain and flake the tuna fish and arrange on top with the prawns. Squeeze over the lemon juice. Sprinkle with the basil and cheeses.

Bake at once in a preheated hot oven, 220°C (425°F), for 15 to 20 minutes, until golden. Serve immediately, garnished with lemon slices if preferred.

Serves 4

ARTICHOKE AND MUSHROOM PIZZA

*1 quantity pizza dough**
2 tablespoons tomato paste
4-6 tomatoes, skinned and sliced
2 tablespoons each chopped basil and oregano
1 × 400 g can artichoke hearts, drained and sliced
60 g (2 oz) button mushrooms, thinly sliced
3 tablespoons olive oil
¼ cup each grated parmesan and matured cheddar cheese

Roll out the dough*. Spread the tomato paste thinly over the base. Arrange the tomatoes on top and sprinkle with the herbs. Place the artichokes and mushrooms on top and drizzle over the oil. Sprinkle with the cheeses.

Slide the pizza onto a hot baking sheet* and bake at once in a preheated hot oven, 220°C (425°F), for 15 to 20 minutes, until golden. Serve immediately.

Serves 4

BAKED VEGETABLE PIZZA

125 g (4 oz) snow peas
60 g (2 oz) green beans
60 g (2 oz) baby carrots, sliced
salt and pepper
4 canned artichoke hearts, drained
30 g (1 oz) butter
¼ cup flour
⅔ cup milk
2 tablespoons cream
¼ cup grated parmesan cheese
½ cup grated matured cheddar cheese
pinch of dried mixed herbs
2 egg yolks
*1 quantity pizza dough**

Blanch the snow peas, beans and carrots in boiling salted water for 3 minutes. Drain and leave to cool.

Cut the beans and snow peas in half and slice the artichokes. Mix all the vegetables together and set aside.

Melt the butter in a pan, add the flour and cook for 2 minutes, without browning. Gradually add the milk, bring to the boil, stirring, and cook for 2 minutes. Remove from the heat, stir in the cream, parmesan cheese, half the cheddar cheese, herbs and egg yolks. Stir in the vegetables.

Roll out the dough*, making the edge at least twice as thick as the rest and 2.5 cm (1 inch) high.

Spoon the sauce into the centre and sprinkle over the remaining cheddar cheese.

Slide the pizza onto a hot baking sheet* and bake at once in a preheated hot oven, 220°C (425°F), for 15 to 20 minutes, until golden.

Leave for 10 minutes before serving.

Serves 4

MEAT AND CHEESE STUFFED PIZZA

4 tablespoons olive oil
1 onion, sliced
250 g (8 oz) minced beef
½ cup dry white wine
1-2 cloves garlic, crushed
salt and pepper
60 g (2 oz) unsmoked ham, diced
90 g (3 oz) matured cheddar cheese, diced
60 g (2 oz) ricotta or curd cheese
*1 quantity pizza dough**
2 tablespoons fresh breadcrumbs, toasted

Heat 3 tablespoons of the oil in a pan, add the onion and cook for about 5 minutes, until golden, stirring occasionally. Add the minced beef and cook until browned, stirring constantly.

Add the wine, lower the heat slightly and cook, uncovered, for about 15 minutes, until all the liquid has reduced. Stir in the garlic, and salt and pepper to taste. Transfer to a bowl and leave to cool completely.

Stir the ham and cheeses into the mixture until very smooth.

Knead the dough on a floured board and divide into 2 unequal pieces. Roll out the larger piece into a 25 to 30 cm (10 to 12 inch) circle and place on a floured piece of circular cardboard. Sprinkle with half the breadcrumbs and cover with the filling, leaving a 1 cm (½ inch) border all round. Sprinkle with the remaining breadcrumbs and 1 tablespoon oil.

Roll out the remaining dough to the same size. Dampen the edges with water and place over the stuffing, pinching the edges together to seal well.

Brush the top with a little water and slide the pizza onto a hot baking sheet*. Bake in a preheated hot oven, 200°C (425°F), for 25 minutes or until golden.

Leave to stand for 30 to 40 minutes. Cut into wedges to serve.

Serves 4 to 6

CHILLI-TOPPED PIZZA

2 tablespoons oil
4 shallots, chopped
½-1 teaspoon chilli powder
250 g (8 oz) minced beef
1 × 400 g can tomatoes
dash of Tabasco sauce
1 × 300 g can red kidney beans
1 clove garlic, crushed
salt and pepper
*1 quantity pizza dough**
125 g (4 oz) Bel Paese cheese, diced
2 teaspoons grated parmesan cheese

Heat the oil in a pan, add the shallots and cook for 2 minutes. Stir in the chilli powder and minced beef and cook until browned, stirring occasionally. Add the tomatoes, with their juice, and Tabasco.

Bring to the boil, cover and simmer for 45 minutes, until very thick, stirring occasionally. Remove from the heat.

Drain and rinse the kidney beans under cold water. Add to the pan with the garlic, and salt and pepper to taste. Leave to cool.

Roll out the dough*. Slide the pizza onto a hot baking sheet* and spoon over the chilli mixture. Sprinkle with the cheeses and bake in a preheated hot oven, 220°C (425°F), for 15 to 20 minutes. Serve immediately.

Serves 4

HAM AND CHEESE PIZZA PIE

30 g (1 oz) butter
3 tomatoes, skinned, seeded and chopped
2 tablespoons dry white wine
6 basil leaves, finely chopped
salt and pepper
*double quantity pizza dough**
125 g (4 oz) mozzarella cheese, sliced
60 g (2 oz) Bel Paese cheese, sliced
185 g (6 oz) smoked back bacon, derinded and cut into thin strips
1/2 cup grated matured cheddar cheese
beaten egg to glaze

Melt the butter in a pan, add the tomatoes and wine, bring to the boil and cook for 5 minutes. Add the basil, and salt and pepper to taste; cool.

When the dough has doubled in size*, place it on a floured board and knead thoroughly. Break off two thirds, roll out into a thin circle and use to line a greased 23 cm (9 inch) loose-bottomed cake tin, ensuring that the dough comes up the side.

Spread the tomato mixture over the base, cover with half the mozzarella and Bel Paese and all the bacon. Lay the remaining cheese slices on top and sprinkle with the cheddar cheese.

Roll out the remaining dough to fit the top of the pizza, dampen the edges and seal well. Leave in a warm place to rise for 30 to 40 minutes.

Brush with beaten egg and bake in a preheated hot oven, 200°C (400°F), for 15 minutes. Lower the heat to 190°C (375°F), and cook for 20 minutes. Serve immediately.
Serves 6

FOUR SEASONS PIZZA

2 tablespoons oil
1 clove garlic, crushed
125 g (4 oz) button mushrooms, sliced
1 tablespoon chopped parsley
1-2 teaspoons capers
60 g (2 oz) peeled prawns
2 rashers streaky bacon, derinded and chopped
2 tablespoons sweetcorn
*1 quantity pizza dough**
½ quantity Tomato Sauce (see American Hot Pizza, page 30)
125 g (4 oz) mozzarella cheese, diced
2 tomatoes, sliced
4 black olives, stoned and halved
1 teaspoon dried mixed herbs

Heat the oil in a pan, add the garlic and mushrooms and cook for 2 minutes. Stir in the parsley and leave to cool.

Mix the capers and prawns together. Mix the bacon and sweetcorn together.

Roll out the dough*. Spread the Tomato Sauce over the base and sprinkle with the cheese. Using a palette knife, gently mark the pizza into quarters.

Arrange the mushrooms on one quarter, the prawns on the another, sprinkle the bacon and sweetcorn on the third quarter, and arrange the tomatoes and olives on the last quarter. Sprinkle the herbs all over.

Slide the pizza onto a hot baking sheet* and bake at once in a preheated hot oven, 220°C (425°F), for 15 to 20 minutes, until golden. Serve immediately.

Serves 4

FRENCH BREAD PIZZA

1 French loaf
2 tablespoons oil
1/4 cup tomato paste
1 teaspoon dried mixed herbs
1-2 cloves garlic, crushed
3 tomatoes, sliced
185 g (6 oz) peeled prawns
125 g (4 oz) mozzarella cheese, grated
2 teaspoons capers
125 g (4 oz) salami, sliced
8 stuffed olives, sliced
125 g (4 oz) gruyère cheese, grated

Cut the bread in half lengthwise, brush the crust with the oil, and spread the tomato paste over the cut surfaces. Sprinkle with the herbs and garlic.

Arrange the tomatoes, prawns and mozzarella cheese on one half. Sprinkle with the capers.

Arrange the salami and olives on the other half. Sprinkle with the gruyère cheese.

Cut each piece of bread into 4. Place on a lightly greased baking sheet and bake in a preheated hot oven, 200°C (400°F), for 12 to 15 minutes. Serve hot.

Serves 4 to 8

ASPARAGUS AND TOMATO PAN PIZZA

¼ cup tomato paste
1 clove garlic, crushed
½ teaspoon each dried basil and oregano
*1 quantity pizza dough**
30 g (1 oz) mozzarella cheese, grated
250 g (8 oz) tomatoes, skinned and sliced
250 g (8 oz) cooked asparagus
90 g (3 oz) Bel Paese cheese, cubed
1 tablespoon chopped thyme (optional)
1 tablespoon grated parmesan cheese

Mix together the tomato paste, garlic and herbs.

Lightly grease a very large heavy-based frying pan. Roll out the dough on a floured board to the size of the pan. Place in the pan and bring a little dough up the sides.

Sprinkle over the mozzarella cheese and spoon the tomato paste mixture on top. Arrange the tomatoes and asparagus over the pizza and sprinkle with the Bel Paese, thyme, if using, and parmesan cheese.

Cook over medium heat for 15 to 20 minutes, then place under a preheated hot grill for 1 to 2 minutes until golden. Serve immediately.

Serves 4

PIZZA TURNOVERS

*1 quantity pizza dough**
olive oil for brushing
4 tomatoes, skinned, seeded and chopped
1 tablespoon chopped basil
6 small slices mozzarella cheese
185 g (6 oz) peeled prawns
¼ cup grated matured cheddar cheese
salt and pepper
oil for deep-frying

Divide the dough into 6 equal pieces. Roll out each piece very thinly into a 15 cm (6 inch) circle, turning the dough to prevent shrinking. Brush the centre of each circle with a little olive oil and the edge with water.

Divide the tomatoes between the circles, placing in the centre, and sprinkle with the basil. Place a slice of mozzarella on top, then the prawns. Sprinkle with the grated cheese and season liberally with salt and pepper.

Fold the dough over the filling to form a crescent and seal the edges well. Place on a floured board, cover with a clean tea-towel and leave to rise in a warm place for 25 to 30 minutes.

Heat the oil in a deep pan, add 2 'turnovers' at a time and cook for 5 to 6 minutes on each side, until golden. Drain on kitchen paper and serve immediately.

Serves 6

MAIN COURSE PASTA DISHES

LASAGNE WITH RICOTTA PESTO

220 g (7 oz) basil leaves
3/4 cup olive oil
90 g (3 oz) pinenuts
4 cloves garlic, roughly chopped
1 2/3 cup grated parmesan cheese
1/4 cup grated matured cheddar cheese
60 g (2 oz) ricotta or curd cheese
salt
60 g (2 oz) butter, softened
*250 g (8 oz) quantity pasta dough**
basil sprigs to garnish

Put the basil, oil, pinenuts and garlic in an electric blender or food processor and work until smooth. Transfer to a bowl and stir in the cheeses and salt to taste. Beat in the butter.

Cut the pasta into 7 × 13 cm (3 × 5 inch) lengths and cook, in two batches, for about 1 minute, until *al dente**. Drain and keep warm.

Add 1 tablespoon of the cooking water to the pesto and mix well.

Arrange a quarter of the lasagne on a warmed serving dish and cover with a quarter of the pesto. Repeat the layers. Garnish with basil and serve immediately.

Serves 4 to 6

SPAGHETTI ALLA CARBONARA

500 g (1 lb) fresh spaghetti
125 g (4 oz) bacon, derinded and chopped
60 g (2 oz) butter
2 cloves garlic, crushed
3 eggs
2/3 cup cream
3/4 cup grated matured cheddar cheese
1/2 cup grated parmesan cheese
1 teaspoon French mustard
salt and pepper
1 tablespoon each chopped thyme and parsley
thyme sprigs to garnish

Cook the spaghetti until *al dente**. Meanwhile fry the bacon in its own fat until crisp. Drain the pasta thoroughly, return to the pan, add the butter and toss well. Stir in the garlic and bacon.

Beat together the eggs, cream, cheeses and mustard. Season with a little salt and plenty of pepper and add the herbs.

Pour the mixture over the spaghetti and stir over a gentle heat until the sauce is creamy, taking care not to 'scramble' the eggs. Transfer to a warmed serving dish and garnish with thyme. Serve immediately, accompanied by parmesan cheese.

Serves 4 to 6

PASTA AND SPINACH ROLL

90 g (3 oz) butter
1 large onion, chopped
60 g (2 oz) ham or prosciutto crudo, diced
500 g (1 lb) frozen leaf spinach, roughly chopped
220 g (7 oz) ricotta or curd cheese
½ cup grated parmesan cheese
little grated nutmeg
1 egg yolk
*250 g (8 oz) quantity pasta dough**
1¼ cups Béchamel sauce (see Baked Rigatoni, page 53)

TOMATO SAUCE:
1 tablespoon olive oil
1 large onion, finely chopped
2 carrots, chopped
2 celery sticks, chopped
1 × 400 g can tomatoes
⅔ cup dry white wine
½ teaspoon dried mixed herbs
salt and pepper

First, make the tomato sauce. Heat the olive oil in a pan, add the onion, carrots and celery and cook for 5 minutes, without browning, stirring occasionally. Add the tomatoes and their juice, the wine, herbs, and salt and pepper to taste. Bring to the boil, cover and simmer for 20 minutes. Remove the lid and cook for 10 to 15 minutes until thickened; set aside.

Melt the butter in a pan, add the onion and cook until golden brown. Lower the heat, stir in the ham and spinach and cook for 5 minutes, stirring occasionally.

Put the ricotta or curd cheese and all but 2 tablespoons of the parmesan cheese in a bowl. Stir in the spinach mixture, and season with salt and pepper to taste. Add the nutmeg and egg yolk.

Roll out the pasta to an oblong shape and cover with the filling, leaving a 2.5 cm (1 inch) border around the edge. Fold in the two ends and roll up like a Swiss roll. Wrap in muslin and tie the ends securely with string.

Cook in boiling salted water for 20 minutes. Remove from the pan, leave to cool then remove the muslin.

Stir the Béchamel sauce into the tomato sauce.

Slice the roll into 1.5 cm (¾ inch) thick slices and arrange in a buttered ovenproof dish. Spoon over the sauce and sprinkle with the reserved parmesan cheese.

Bake uncovered in a preheated hot oven, 200°C (400°F), for 15 to 20 minutes. Garnish with fresh herbs if liked, and serve immediately.

Serves 4 to 6

NOTE: If you do not have a large enough pan, make 2 smaller rolls.

PASTA WITH SQUID AND TOMATO

375 g (12 oz) squid, cut into 5 mm (1/4 inch) strips
2/3 cup dry white wine
1 bouquet garni
6 tablespoons olive oil
1 large onion, chopped
750 g (1 1/2 lb) tomatoes, skinned, seeded and chopped
2 tablespoons chopped basil
1 tablespoon chopped parsley
salt and pepper
1-2 cloves garlic, crushed
500 g (1 lb) fresh tagliatelle
30 g (1 oz) butter
parsley sprigs to garnish

Place the squid in a shallow pan with the wine and bouquet garni. Bring to the boil, cover and simmer for 2 minutes. Using a slotted spoon, remove the squid and set aside. Discard the bouquet garni. Reserve the cooking liquid.

Heat the oil in a pan, add the onion and cook for 5 minutes, without browning. Stir in the tomatoes, herbs, and salt and pepper to taste. Strain the reserved liquid into the pan, bring to the boil, cover and simmer for 30 minutes. Add the garlic and boil, for about 5 minutes, until reduced and thickened.

Meanwhile, cook the tagliatelle until *al dente**. Drain thoroughly and turn into a warmed serving dish. Add the butter and toss well. Add the squid to the sauce, heat through, pour over the pasta and serve immediately, garnished with parsley.

Serves 4 to 6

PASTA WITH BABY VEGETABLES

3 tablespoons dry white wine
1 tablespoon chopped chervil
2 tablespoons cream
185 g (6 oz) butter
125 g (4 oz) mushrooms, sliced
2 tomatoes, skinned, seeded and chopped
salt and pepper
1 teaspoon lemon juice
2 tablespoons olive oil
155 g (5 oz) cauliflower florets
1 small zucchini, thinly sliced
60 g (2 oz) snow peas
4 canned artichoke hearts, drained and quartered
60 g (2 oz) peas
375 g (12 oz) dried spaghetti

Put the wine and chervil in a pan, bring to the boil and boil steadily until reduced by half. Add the cream, 155 g (5 oz) of the butter in small pieces, the mushrooms and tomatoes. Season well with salt and pepper. Bring to the boil and boil for 30 seconds. Stir in the lemon juice.

Heat the olive oil in a large frying pan or wok, add all the remaining vegetables and stir-fry for 2 to 3 minutes.

Meanwhile, cook the spaghetti until *al dente**. Drain well and toss in the remaining butter. Spoon over the mushroom sauce and toss well.

Transfer to a warmed serving plate, surround with the vegetables and serve immediately.

Serves 4

TORTELLINI WITH RICOTTA AND SPINACH SAUCE

125 g (4 oz) butter
250 g (8 oz) frozen leaf spinach, thawed and chopped
salt and pepper
500 g (1 lb) fresh tortellini
125 g (4 oz) ricotta or curd cheese
½ cup grated parmesan cheese

Heat half the butter in a large frying pan, add the spinach and toss thoroughly. Season well with salt and pepper. Sauté the spinach for 2 minutes, stirring constantly.

Cook the tortellini until *al dente**. Drain thoroughly and toss in the remaining butter.

Stir the ricotta cheese and half of the parmesan into the spinach mixture, then stir in the pasta. Transfer to a warmed serving dish, sprinkle with the remaining parmesan and serve immediately.

Serves 4

CHICKEN AND NUTS WITH NOODLES

500 g (1 lb) chicken breast
2 tablespoons soy sauce
4 tablespoons dry sherry
3/4 cup unsalted peanuts
3 tablespoons oil
1 bunch green shallots, chopped
2 cloves garlic, thinly sliced
1 cm (1/2 inch) piece fresh root ginger, chopped
3 tablespoons Hoi Sin sauce (Chinese plum sauce)
375 g (12 oz) dried vermicelli
salt
green shallots to garnish

Cut the chicken into 2.5 cm (1 inch) pieces. Place in a bowl, pour over the soy sauce and sherry and mix well. Cover and leave for 30 minutes.

Put the nuts on a baking tray and place in a preheated moderate oven, 180°C (350°F), for 8 to 10 minutes until brown.

Heat the oil in a wok or large frying pan, add the green shallots, garlic and ginger and cook, without browning, for 1 minute. Add the chicken and marinade, increase the heat and cook for 10 to 12 minutes, stirring occasionally. Stir in the Hoi Sin sauce.

Cook the vermicelli until *al dente**; drain thoroughly. Add to the pan and cook for a further 2 minutes. Transfer to a warmed serving dish and serve immediately, garnished with green shallots.

Serves 4

TRADITIONAL MACARONI CHEESE

250 g (8 oz) dried short-cut macaroni
60 g (2 oz) butter
¼ cup plain flour
1¾ cups milk
1 heaped teaspoon English mustard
dash of Tabasco sauce
dash of Worcestershire sauce
1½ cups grated matured cheddar cheese
¼ cup dried breadcrumbs
¼ cup grated parmesan cheese
2 tomatoes, sliced

Cook the macaroni until *al dente**; drain thoroughly, then toss in half the butter.

Heat the remaining butter in a pan, stir in the flour and cook, stirring, for 2 minutes, without browning. Gradually add the milk and bring to the boil, stirring constantly. Cook for 2 minutes, then stir in the mustard, and Tabasco and Worcestershire sauces. Add the cheddar cheese and stir until melted. Fold in the macaroni.

Spoon into a buttered ovenproof dish and sprinkle with the breadcrumbs and parmesan cheese.

Bake in a preheated hot oven, 200°C (400°F), for 25 to 30 minutes. Arrange the tomato slices on top, return to the oven for 5 to 10 minutes, until hot and golden brown. Serve immediately.

Serves 4

GARLIC CHICKEN WITH NOODLES

2 tablespoons oil
90 g (3 oz) butter
1 large onion, finely chopped
500 g (1 lb) boned chicken breasts
2-3 garlic bulbs, broken into cloves
1¼ cups dry white wine
1 teaspoon chopped tarragon
salt and pepper
125 g (4 oz) button mushrooms, sliced
4 tablespoons chopped parsley
500 g (1 lb) fresh tagliatelle verdi or noodles
¼ cup dried breadcrumbs
¼ cup grated parmesan cheese
tarragon sprigs to garnish

Heat the oil and 60 g (2 oz) of the butter in a pan, add the onion and cook for 2 minutes, until transparent.

Cut the chicken into 5 cm (2 inch) pieces, add to the pan and brown on all sidcs. Add thc garlic, winc, tarragon, and salt and pepper to taste, bring to the boil, cover and simmer for 30 minutes. Remove the garlic, stir in the mushrooms and cook for 2 minutes. Stir in the parsley.

Cook the pasta until *al dente**; drain thoroughly and toss in the remaining butter.

Mix the sauce and noodles together, spoon into a buttered ovenproof dish, and sprinkle with the breadcrumbs and parmesan cheese. Bake in a preheated hot oven, 200°C (400°C), for 20 to 25 minutes, until hot and golden brown.

Garnish with tarragon, and serve immediately.

Serves 4 to 6

PASTA WITH CHICKEN LIVERS

1 tablespoon oil
60 g (2 oz) butter
4 shallots, chopped
4 rashers back bacon, derinded and chopped
250 g (8 oz) minced beef
⅔ cup each dry vermouth and dry white wine
375 g (12 oz) tomatoes, skinned, seeded and chopped
salt and pepper
2 cloves garlic, crushed
2 tablespoons each chopped parsley, marjoram and sage
250 g (8 oz) chicken livers, chopped
500 g (1 lb) dried pasta spirals or shells

Heat the oil and half the butter in a pan, add the shallots and cook, stirring constantly, for 2 to 3 minutes, without browning. Add the bacon and minced beef, increase the heat and brown quickly, stirring.

Add the vermouth and wine and boil rapidly for 15 minutes. Stir in the tomatoes and season well with salt and pepper. Stir in the garlic and herbs. Add the chicken livers and cook for 3 minutes.

Cook the pasta until *al dente**. Drain thoroughly, turn into a warmed serving dish, add the remaining butter and toss well.

Spoon the sauce over the pasta and toss well. Garnish with sage or parsley if liked, and serve immediately.

Serves 6

NOODLES WITH BROCCOLI, MUSHROOMS AND SHELLFISH

1 head of broccoli
2 tablespoons olive oil
1 tablespoon chopped fresh ginger
2 cloves garlic, thinly sliced
125 g (4 oz) button mushrooms, sliced
250 g (8 oz) scallops
185 g (6 oz) peeled prawns
⅔ cup dry sherry
1¼ cups cream
1 teaspoon each chopped marjoram and thyme
1 tablespoon parsley
salt and pepper
500 g (1 lb) fresh tagliatelle verdi

Break the broccoli into florets and boil for 1 minute; leave to cool.

Heat the oil in a wok or large frying pan, add the ginger and garlic and brown lightly. Stir in the mushrooms, scallops and prawns. Pour over the sherry. Boil rapidly until the liquid has reduced to about 2 tablespoons. Add the cream, herbs, and salt and pepper to taste.

Meanwhile, cook the tagliatelle until *al dente**; drain thoroughly.

Add the broccoli to the sauce, check the seasoning and heat through.

Transfer the tagliatelle to a warmed serving dish, pour over the sauce and serve immediately.

Serves 4 to 6

SPAGHETTI AL TONNO

4 tablespoons olive oil
2-3 cloves garlic, crushed
1 kg (2 lb) tomatoes, skinned, seeded and chopped
1 tablespoon each chopped basil and oregano
salt and pepper
2 × 200 g cans tuna fish, drained and flaked
1 teaspoon anchovy essence
2 teaspoons capers (optional)
500 g (1 lb) fresh spaghetti
30 g (1 oz) butter
oregano or basil sprigs to garnish (optional)

Heat the oil in a pan, add the garlic and cook until golden brown, stirring occasionally. Add the tomatoes, herbs, and pepper to taste. Bring to the boil and simmer, uncovered, for 30 minutes, until thickened. Add the tuna, anchovy essence and capers, if using.

Cook the spaghetti until *al dente**. Drain thoroughly, turn into a warmed serving dish, add the butter and toss well.

Taste the sauce and add salt if necessary, then spoon over the pasta. Garnish with oregano or basil if liked, and serve immediately.

Serves 4 to 6

SPAGHETTI WITH MUSSELS

1 kg (2 lb) fresh mussels
4 tablespoons olive oil
90 g (3 oz) butter
2-3 cloves garlic, crushed
1 large onion, finely chopped
750 g (1½ lb) tomatoes, skinned, seeded and chopped
⅔ cup dry white wine
1 teaspoon dried mixed herbs
salt and pepper
500 g (1 lb) fresh spaghetti
chopped parsley to garnish

Put the mussels in a large pan, cover and bring to the boil without water. Cook for 5 to 6 minutes, until the shells have opened. Reserve 4 tablespoons liquid. Drain the mussels, discarding any that have not opened.

Heat the oil and 30 g (1 oz) of the butter in a pan, add the garlic and onion and cook for 5 minutes, until pale golden. Add the tomatoes, wine, herbs, salt and pepper to taste, and the reserved cooking liquid. Bring to the boil and cook, uncovered, for 30 minutes, until thickened.

Meanwhile, cook the spaghetti until *al dente**. Drain thoroughly and turn into a warmed serving dish. Add the remaining butter and toss well.

Add the mussels to the sauce and heat through. Pour over the pasta, sprinkle with chopped parsley and serve immediately.

Serves 4 to 6

BAKED RIGATONI WITH MEAT SAUCE

2 tablespoons oil
60 g (2 oz) butter
1 onion, chopped
2 celery sticks, chopped
2 carrots, chopped
375 g (12 oz) minced beef
salt and pepper
1¼ cups dry white wine
6 tablespoons milk
little grated nutmeg
1-2 cloves garlic, crushed
1 × 400 g can tomatoes, chopped
500 g (1 lb) dried rigatoni or penne
45 g (1½ oz) butter
6 tablespoons grated parmesan cheese

BECHAMEL SAUCE:

1¾ cups milk
1 carrot
1 onion
3-4 peppercorns
1 bay leaf
60 g (2 oz) butter
60 g (2 oz) plain flour

Heat the oil and butter in a pan, add the onion, celery and carrots and cook for 2 minutes, without browning. Increase the heat, add the minced beef and brown well. Season liberally with salt and pepper, add the wine and cook rapidly until it has evaporated.

Lower the heat, add the milk and cook until it has reduced completely.

Stir in the nutmeg, garlic and tomatoes with their juice. Cover and simmer for 1 to 1½ hours, stirring occasionally. Check the seasoning.

Meanwhile, make the Béchamel sauce. Put the milk, carrot, onion, peppercorns and bay leaf in a pan and bring to the boil slowly. Turn off the heat, leave to cool, then strain.

Melt the butter in a pan, add the flour and cook for 1 minute, without browning. Gradually add the strained milk, stirring constantly. Bring to the boil and cook for 2 minutes. Season with salt and pepper to taste.

Cook the pasta until just *al dente**. Drain, place in a large bowl with the butter and toss well. Pour over the meat and Béchamel sauces, and 4 tablespoons of the parmesan cheese; mix well.

Transfer to a buttered ovenproof dish, sprinkle with the remaining cheese and bake in a preheated hot oven, 200°C (400°F), for 20 to 25 minutes until hot and golden brown. Serve immediately.

Serves 6

CAPPELLETTI WITH FISH STUFFING AND SHRIMP SAUCE

1 small onion, halved
1 celery stick, roughly chopped
1 small carrot, roughly chopped
375 g (12 oz) gemfish or other white fish, skin removed
¾ cup dry white wine
salt and pepper
2 egg yolks
¼ cup grated parmesan cheese
1 teaspoon chopped marjoram
pinch of grated nutmeg
*250 g (8 oz) quantity pasta dough**
30 g (1 oz) butter

SAUCE:

4 tablespoons olive oil
2 cloves garlic, crushed
8 tomatoes, skinned, seeded and chopped
4 tablespoons dry white wine
250 g (8 oz) peeled prawns, chopped
1¼ cups cream
2 tablespoons chopped parsley

TO GARNISH:

parsley and marjoram sprigs

Put the onion, celery, carrot and fish in a frying pan, pour over the wine and season well with salt and pepper. Bring to the boil and simmer for 10 minutes, until the fish is tender. Drain and flake the fish into a bowl. Add the egg yolks, cheese, marjoram and nutmeg. Mix well and season with salt and pepper to taste.

Cut the pasta dough into 3.5 cm (1½ inch) squares. Place ½ teaspoon of filling in the centre of each square and dampen the edges of the dough with water. With one corner facing you, fold into a triangle and seal the edges. Then take the left and right corners together to form a circle and pinch to seal. Place the cappelletti on a clean dry tea-towel and leave to dry for 1 hour.

Meanwhile, make the sauce. Put the oil and garlic in a pan and cook for 2 to 3 minutes, until the garlic is golden brown. Add the tomatoes and wine, bring to the boil and simmer, uncovered, for 15 to 20 minutes, until thickened. Stir in the prawns and season with salt and pepper to taste.

Add the cream and gradually bring to the boil, stirring constantly. Stir in the parsley and remove from the heat.

Cook the cappelletti for 30 seconds to 1 minute, until *al dente**. Drain thoroughly and transfer to a warmed serving dish. Add the butter, toss well, then pour over the sauce. Garnish with parsley and marjoram and serve immediately.

Serves 4

SEAFOOD PASTA

4 fillets of bream, skinned, with bones
1¼ cups dry white wine
1 small onion, halved
½ teaspoon dried mixed herbs
60 g (2 oz) butter
1 clove garlic, crushed
2 shallots, chopped
8 scallops
4 large tomatoes, skinned, seeded and chopped
1 teaspoon chopped basil
2 tablespoons chopped parsley
⅔ cup cream
salt and pepper
500 g (1 lb) fresh egg noodles or tagliatelle
250 g (8 oz) peeled prawns
whole prawns to garnish

Place the skin and bones from the fish in a pan with the wine, onion and herbs. Simmer, uncovered, for 20 minutes. Cool and strain.

Melt half the butter in a pan, add the garlic and shallots and cook for 5 minutes. Cut the fish into 5 cm (2 inch) pieces and add to the pan with the fish stock. Bring to the boil, simmer for 2 minutes, remove the fish and set aside. Add the white part of the scallops and cook for 30 seconds, add the coral part and cook for just under 30 seconds; remove.

Boil the liquid until reduced to 2 tablespoons. Add the tomatoes and basil and cook for 10 minutes, stirring occasionally, until thickened. Stir in the parsley, cream, and salt and pepper to taste.

Cook the noodles until *al dente**. Drain and turn into a warmed serving dish. Add the remaining butter and toss well. Add the prawns and fish to the sauce, bring to the boil, then pour over the noodles. Serve immediately, garnished with whole prawns.

Serves 4

HAM AND MUSHROOM LASAGNE

4 tablespoons oil
90 g (3 oz) butter
1 small onion, chopped
1¼ cups dry white wine
3 large tomatoes, skinned, seeded and chopped
750 g (1½ lb) button mushrooms, sliced
1-2 cloves garlic, crushed
1 teaspoon dried mixed herbs
2 tablespoons chopped parsley
salt and pepper
315 g (10 oz) dried lasagne
1¾ cups Béchamel sauce (see Baked Rigatoni, page 53)
375 g (12 oz) unsmoked ham, in thin strips
1 × 400 g can artichoke hearts, drained and sliced
½ cup grated parmesan cheese

Heat the oil and butter in a pan, add the onion and cook for 2 minutes. Add the wine and tomatoes, bring to the boil and simmer for 20 minutes, stirring occasionally, until the liquid has evaporated.

Stir in the mushrooms, garlic and herbs and cook for 6 to 7 minutes, until thickened. Add the parsley, and salt and pepper to taste.

Cook the lasagne until *al dente**. Drain and cool under cold running water, then drain thoroughly.

Line the base of a large buttered ovenproof dish with lasagne. Spoon over some mushrooms, then a little Béchamel sauce. Sprinkle with ham and artichoke. Repeat the layers, finishing with pasta and Béchamel sauce.

Sprinkle with the parmesan and bake in a preheated hot oven, 200°C (400°F), for 20 to 25 minutes until golden brown. Serve immediately.
Serves 6

SALAD ACCOMPANIMENTS

AVOCADO AND MUSHROOM SALAD

250 g (8 oz) button mushrooms, sliced
½ head of curly endive
1 lime or lemon
2 large avocados
2 tablespoons pinenuts, toasted

DRESSING:
6 tablespoons olive oil
3-4 tablespoons lime juice
1 teaspoon finely grated lemon rind
1 clove garlic, crushed
1 teaspoon crushed coriander seeds
1 teaspoon honey
salt and pepper

Mix the dressing ingredients together, seasoning with salt and pepper to taste. Put the mushrooms in a large bowl, pour over the dressing and toss well, until all the mushrooms are coated.

Arrange the endive on a flat plate. Squeeze the juice from half of the lime or lemon; slice the remainder. Slice the avocados and sprinkle with the lime or lemon juice to prevent browning. Arrange on top of the endive.

Spoon the mushrooms in the centre. Sprinkle the pinenuts over the salad, and garnish with the lime or lemon slices. Serve immediately.
Serves 4

COUNTRY GARDEN SALAD

250 g (8 oz) very small new potatoes
salt and pepper
mint sprig
250 g (8 oz) new carrots, quartered lengthwise
250 g (8 oz) peas
125 g (4 oz) small green beans
1 thin leek, blanched and sliced

DRESSING:
4 tablespoons olive oil
2 tablespoons lemon juice
1 teaspoon Dijon mustard
½ teaspoon honey
1 clove garlic, crushed
2 tablespoons chopped mint

Cook the potatoes in boiling salted water with a sprig of mint for 10 to 12 minutes, until tender. Drain and cool under running cold water. Drain thoroughly.

Cook the carrots in boiling salted water for 7 to 10 minutes, add the peas and beans to the pan and cook for a further 3 minutes. Drain the vegetables and cool under running cold water. Drain thoroughly.

Put the cooked vegetables in a large bowl and add the leek.

Mix the dressing ingredients together, seasoning with salt and pepper to taste. Spoon over the vegetables and mix well.

Pile the salad into a salad bowl and serve immediately.

Serves 4

GREEN BEAN AND HAZELNUT SALAD

500 g (1 lb) small green beans
salt and pepper
¼ cup shelled hazelnuts
few lettuce leaves
DRESSING:
1 teaspoon Dijon mustard
finely grated rind of ½ lemon
juice of 1 lemon
7-8 tablespoons cream, lightly whipped

Cook the beans in boiling salted water for 4 to 5 minutes, until just tender. Drain, cool under cold running water. Drain thoroughly. Cut the hazelnuts into thin slices. Place under a moderate grill until golden.

Mix the dressing ingredients together in a large bowl, add the beans and toss well. Season with salt and pepper to taste.

Arrange the lettuce on a serving dish. Pile the beans in the centre and sprinkle over the nuts. Garnish with fresh herbs as liked, and serve immediately.

Serves 4

CONTINENTAL SUMMER SALAD

4 carrots, grated
1 tablespoon chopped parsley
2 small fennel bulbs, sliced
juice of ½ lemon
1 tablespoon chopped thyme
2 large tomatoes
125 g (4 oz) mozzarella cheese
185 g (6 oz) English spinach
1 head of radicchio
½ cup salted cashew nuts
DRESSING:
6 tablespoons olive oil
3 tablespoons lemon juice
1 teaspoon each grated lemon rind, French mustard and honey
1-2 cloves garlic, crushed
3 tablespoons chopped basil
salt and pepper

Mix together the carrots and parsley and set aside.

Mix the fennel, lemon juice and thyme together.

Arrange the carrots on one quarter of a large platter, the fennel on the next quarter.

Slice the tomatoes and mozzarella and arrange alternately in the third quarter.

Tear the spinach and radicchio leaves into pieces and arrange on the remaining quarter of the platter. Sprinkle with the nuts.

Mix the dressing ingredients together, seasoning with salt and pepper to taste. Spoon over the salad and serve immediately.

Serves 4

NOTE: This dish is also suitable to serve as an hors d'oeuvre.

ZUCCHINI AND BACON SALAD

500 g (1 lb) baby zucchini
2 spring onions
185 g (6 oz) streaky bacon, derinded
2 hard-boiled egg yolks, sieved

DRESSING:
6 tablespoons olive oil
3 tablespoons lemon juice
1 teaspoon honey
1 teaspoon coarse grain mustard
1-2 cloves garlic, crushed
2 tablespoons each chopped marjoram and thyme
salt and pepper

TO GARNISH *(optional)*:
marjoram and thyme sprigs

Slice the zucchini very thinly and arrange on a plate. Chop the spring onions finely and sprinkle on top.

Mix the dressing ingredients together, seasoning with salt and pepper to taste. Spoon over the zucchini and set aside.

Grill the bacon until crisp and golden brown, cool and crumble into pieces.

Sprinkle the egg yolk and bacon over the salad, garnish with marjoram and thyme sprigs if liked, and serve immediately.

Serves 4

MOZZARELLA SALAD

3 large tomatoes
1/4 cucumber
1 red and 1 green pepper, cored and seeded
2-3 young zucchini
250 g (8 oz) mozzarella cheese
4 green shallots, chopped
DRESSING:
6 tablespons olive oil
3-4 tablespoons lime juice
1-2 cloves garlic, crushed
1 teaspoon each honey and French mustard
1 tablespoon each chopped parsley, basil and marjoram
1-2 teaspoons green peppercorns (optional)
salt
TO GARNISH:
basil sprigs

Thinly slice the tomatoes, cucumber, peppers, zucchini and cheese and arrange on a flat serving platter, as illustrated. Sprinkle with the green shallots.

Mix the dressing ingredients together, seasoning with salt to taste. Spoon over the salad, cover and chill for 30 minutes. Remove from the refrigerator 15 minutes before required.

Garnish with basil sprigs to serve.

Serves 4 to 6

CLASSIC GREEN SALAD

1 small lettuce
¼ cucumber, sliced
1 green pepper, cored, seeded and sliced
1 bunch watercress
4 green shallots, chopped
2 celery sticks, chopped
1 head of chicory, chopped
2 tablespoons each chopped thyme and marjoram
little mustard and cress
DRESSING:
60 g (2 oz) each Roquefort, Stilton and cream cheese
¾ cup natural yogurt
2 tablespoons mayonnaise
dash of Tabasco sauce
salt and pepper
2 tablespoons snipped chives

First, make the dressing. Cream the cheeses together in a mixing bowl, then gradually stir in the yogurt and mayonnaise. Add the Tabasco, and season with salt and pepper to taste. Stir in the chives. If the dressing is too thick, add a little cold water.

Tear the lettuce into pieces and arrange in a large salad bowl with the cucumber, pepper and watercress. Chop the green shallots, celery and chicory and add to the salad bowl; toss well. Sprinkle over the herbs and spoon sufficient dressing onto the salad to coat it lightly.

Sprinkle with the mustard and cress and serve immediately.

Serves 4 to 6

NOTE: Any remaining dressing will keep in the refrigerator for 4 to 5 days in a covered container.

FRENCH VEGETABLE SALAD

250 g (8 oz) snow peas
125 g (4 oz) young green beans
salt and pepper
1 fennel bulb
3 tablespoons lemon juice
4 tomatoes, quartered
1/4 cucumber, diced
250 g (8 oz) peeled prawns
few stuffed olives
DRESSING:
1-2 cloves garlic, crushed
1/2 teaspoon Dijon mustard
dash each of Tabasco and Worcestershire sauce
6 tablespoons mayonnaise
6 anchovy fillets, finely chopped
1 tablespoon each chopped parsley and chives

Blanch the snow peas and beans for 2 minutes in boiling salted water. Drain and cool under cold running water. Drain thoroughly.

Slice the fennel and toss in the lemon juice; set aside a few feathery leaves for garnish.

Put the snow peas, beans, tomatoes, and fennel with the lemon juice in a large bowl. Stir in the cucumber and prawns.

Mix the dressing ingredients together, seasoning with salt and pepper to taste. Pour over the salad and toss well.

Pile the salad in a bowl, garnish with the stuffed olives and fennel leaves and serve immediately.

Serves 4

ITALIAN CAULIFLOWER SALAD

1 large cauliflower
2 spring onions
125 g (4 oz) Italian salami, diced
125 g (4 oz) mortadella, diced
2 tablespoons black olives
DRESSING:
2 tomatoes
1 canned pimiento
4 tablespoons mayonnaise
1 clove garlic, crushed (optional)
6-8 green olives, stoned and chopped
salt and pepper
TO GARNISH *(optional):*
marjoram sprigs

Break the cauliflower into small florets and chop the spring onions. Place in a bowl with the salami and mortadella.

To make the dressing, skin, seed and chop the tomatoes, and finely chop the pimiento. Put the mayonnaise in a bowl, stir in the tomatoes, pimiento, garlic, if using, and green olives, and season with salt and pepper to taste. Spoon over the salad and mix well.

Arrange in a serving dish, sprinkle with the black olives and garnish with marjoram sprigs if available.

Serves 4

ENDIVE AND BACON SALAD

185 g (6 oz) streaky bacon, derinded
3 thick slices stale bread
oil for deep-frying
1 large head of curly endive
2 heads of radicchio
1-2 avocados
juice of 1 lemon
1-2 hard-boiled eggs
1 tablespoon chopped parsley
DRESSING:
6 tablespoons olive oil
3 tablespoons lemon juice
1-2 teaspoons coarse grain mustard
1-2 cloves garlic, crushed
1 teaspoon honey
salt and pepper

Grill the bacon until crisp and golden brown, cool and crumble into pieces.

Remove the crusts, then cut the bread into cubes or rounds. Heat the oil in a pan, add the croûtons and fry until golden brown. Drain on kitchen paper.

Separate the endive and radicchio into leaves, tear into pieces and place in a deep bowl. Roughly chop the avocado and toss in the lemon juice. Drain and add to the salad with the bacon and croûtons.

Chop the egg white, sieve the yolk, and sprinkle over the salad.

Mix the dressing ingredients together, seasoning with salt and pepper to taste, pour over the salad and toss well. Sprinkle with the parsley and serve immediately.

Serves 4

TUNA AND BEAN SALAD

1 × 440 g can red kidney beans
1 × 300 g can cannellini beans
2-3 celery sticks
2-3 large spring onions
2 heads of radicchio
1 × 200 g can tuna fish, drained and flaked
1 bunch watercress
2 large slices stale bread
oil for deep-frying
DRESSING:
6 tablespoons olive oil
3 tablespoons lime or lemon juice
1-2 cloves garlic, crushed
1 teaspoon honey
2 tablespoons snipped chives
2 tablespoons chopped parsley
salt and pepper

Drain the beans, rinse in a colander under cold running water and drain well. Place in a bowl.

Thinly slice the celery, chop the spring onions, and tear the radicchio leaves into pieces. Add to the beans with the tuna fish.

Mix the dressing ingredients together, seasoning with salt and pepper to taste. Pour over the salad and mix well.

Arrange the watercress in a serving dish and spoon the salad into the centre.

Remove the crusts and cut the bread into cubes or crescent shapes, using small cutters. Heat the oil in a pan, add the croûtons and fry until golden. Drain on kitchen paper. Sprinkle over the salad and serve immediately.

Serves 4

RED AND WHITE COLESLAW

¼ white cabbage
¼ red cabbage
3 celery sticks
2 green shallots, sliced
2 large red apples
juice of 1 lemon
½ cup dates, stoned and chopped
¼ cup walnuts, roughly chopped
¼ cup flaked almonds, toasted
½ cup salted cashew nuts
1 tablespoon chopped coriander or parsley

DRESSING:
6 tablespoons mayonnaise
2 teaspoons lemon juice
1 teaspoon finely grated lemon rind
1 teaspoon green peppercorn mustard
1 tablespoon each chopped parsley and chives
1 clove garlic, crushed
salt

Finely shred the cabbage and thinly slice the celery. Mix the cabbage, celery and shallots together in a large bowl.

Core and slice the apples, toss in the lemon juice, then drain. Stir the apple into the salad. Add the dates and nuts and mix well.

Mix the dressing ingredients together, seasoning with salt to taste. Pile the salad into a large serving bowl and stir in the dressing. Sprinkle with the chopped coriander or parsley.

Garnish with coriander or parsley leaves if liked, and serve immediately.

Serves 4 to 6

PASTA SALADS

These salads can be served as main courses, starters, or accompaniments to grilled meat or fish. Follow the serving guide for each recipe accordingly, ie serving as a main course to the smaller number.

HERBY MACARONI SALAD

500 g (1 lb) dried macaroni
1 red pepper, cored, seeded and diced
1/2 cucumber, diced
3/4 cup natural yogurt
1-2 cloves garlic, crushed
1 tablespoon each chopped parsley, basil, thyme, tarragon, chives, mint and dill
185 g (6 oz) streaky bacon, derinded
1/2 cup salted peanuts

Cook the macaroni until *al dente**. Drain and cool quickly under running cold water. Drain thoroughly and place in a large bowl. Stir in the red pepper, cucumber, yogurt, garlic and herbs. Transfer to a salad bowl.

Fry the bacon in its own fat until crisp, then chop into pieces and sprinkle over the salad with the peanuts.

Garnish with herbs sprigs if liked, and serve immediately.

Serves 4 to 6

PRAWN, AVOCADO AND PASTA SALAD

500 g (1 lb) peeled prawns
315 g (10 oz) dried pasta twists
2 avocados, sliced
1 tablespoon each chopped thyme, marjoram, basil and parsley

DRESSING:

1 clove garlic, crushed
½ teaspoon French mustard
6 tablespoons olive oil
3 tablespoons lemon juice
1 teaspoon finely grated lemon rind
1 teaspoon honey
salt and pepper

TO GARNISH:

black olives
thyme and marjoram sprigs (optional)

Mix the dressing ingredients together in a large bowl, adding salt and pepper to taste. Stir in the prawns, cover and chill for 30 minutes.

Cook the pasta until *al dente**.

Drain and cool quickly under cold running water. Drain thoroughly and add to the prawns. Carefully stir in the avocados and herbs.

Transfer the salad to a serving dish and garnish with black olives, and thyme and marjoram if liked. Serve immediately.

Serves 4 to 8

FENNEL AND PASTA SALAD

500 g (1 lb) dried pasta shells or bows
3 large fennel bulbs, sliced
2-3 red eating apples, cored and sliced
juice of 1 lemon
4 green shallots
4 tomatoes
2 tablespoons sesame seeds toasted
½ cup salted cashew nuts
DRESSING:
6 tablespoons olive oil
3 tablespoons lemon juice
1 teaspoon each French mustard and honey
1 tablespoon each chopped parsley and basil

Cook the pasta until *al dente**. Drain and cool quickly under cold running water. Drain thoroughly and place in a large bowl.

Toss the fennel and apples in the lemon juice, then add to the pasta. Chop the green shallots and skin, seed and chop the tomatoes. Add to the pasta.

Mix the dressing ingredients together and pour over the salad. Transfer to a serving bowl. Sprinkle with the sesame seeds and cashew nuts and garnish with fennel leaves, if liked. Serve immediately.

Serves 4 to 6

PASTA COLESLAW

500 g (1 lb) dried pasta twists or shells
1/4-1/2 small red cabbage, shredded
1 onion, sliced
1/4 cucumber, diced
2 celery sticks, chopped
2 green eating apples, cored and sliced
juice of 1 lemon
1 bunch of watercress
oil for shallow-frying
4 cloves garlic
2 slices stale bread, cubed
DRESSING:
3/4 cup natural yogurt
1-2 cloves garlic, crushed
2 tablespoons each chopped parsley and chives

Cook the pasta until *al dente**. Drain and cool quickly under cold running water. Drain thoroughly and place in a large bowl. Stir in the cabbage, onion, cucumber and celery.

Toss the apple slices in the lemon juice and add to the bowl with the watercress.

Mix the dressing ingredients together and fold into the salad. Transfer to a serving dish.

Heat the oil in a pan, add the garlic cloves and fry until brown; discard. Add the bread cubes and fry until golden. Drain on kitchen paper and sprinkle over the salad. Serve immediately.

Serves 4 to 8

WINTER SALAD

500 g (1 lb) dried tagliatelle verdi
4 celery sticks
1 red pepper
4 red eating apples
juice of 1 lemon
¼-½ green or white cabbage, shredded
125 g (4 oz) black olives
30 g (1 oz) gherkins, sliced
¼ cup sunflower seeds, toasted (optional)

DRESSING:
4-6 tablespoons mayonnaise
2 tablespoons French mustard
1 teaspoon lemon juice
1 clove garlic, crushed
2 tablespoons each chopped parsley and chives
1-2 tablespoons capers, drained

Cook the tagliatelle until *al dente**. Drain and cool quickly under cold running water. Drain thoroughly and place in a large bowl.

Slice the celery and core, seed and slice the red pepper. Add to the tagliatelle.

Core and slice the apples and toss in the lemon juice. Add to the salad with the cabbage.

Mix the dressing ingredients together and carefully mix into the salad with the olives and gherkins.

Transfer to a serving dish and sprinkle with the sunflower seeds, if using. Serve immediately.

Serves 4 to 8

GREEN SALAD WITH NOODLES

⅔ cup oil
500 g (1 lb) fresh egg noodles
125 g (4 oz) streaky bacon, derinded
½ head of curly endive
1 cos lettuce
250 g (8 oz) English spinach
1 bunch of watercress
1 bunch of green shallots, sliced
2 avocados
1 hard-boiled egg
DRESSING:
6 tablespoons olive oil
3 tablespoons lemon juice
1-2 cloves garlic, crushed
½ teaspoon tarragon or herb mustard
1 teaspoon honey
1 tablespoon each chopped marjoram, parsley and thyme

Heat the oil in a wok or large frying pan, add the noodles in batches and fry until golden. Drain on kitchen paper and set aside.

Fry the bacon in its own fat until crisp. Crumble and set aside.

Tear the endive, lettuce and spinach leaves into pieces and place in a deep serving bowl with the watercress and green shallots. Slice the avocados and add to the bowl with the noodles.

Mix the dressing ingredients together, pour over the salad and toss well.

Chop the egg white and sieve the yolk and sprinkle over the salad with the bacon. Serve immediately.

Serves 4 to 6

CHICORY, ORANGE AND PASTA SALAD

500 g (1 lb) fresh tagliatelle
4 heads of chicory, sliced
6 large oranges, segmented
2 tablespoons chopped tarragon
4 tablespoons snipped chives

DRESSING:
6 tablespoons olive oil
2 tablespoons each orange and lemon juice
½ teaspoon coarse-grain mustard
1 teaspoon each honey, mixed herbs and finely grated orange rind

Cut the tagliatelle into shorter lengths and cook until *al dente**. Drain and cool quickly under cold running water. Drain thoroughly and place in a large bowl.

Mix the dressing ingredients together and pour over the pasta.

Stir in the chicory, orange segments and herbs. Transfer to a serving dish and serve immediately.

Serves 4 to 6

PASTA AND BROAD BEAN SALAD

500 g (1 lb) shelled broad beans
salt
500 g (1 lb) dried pasta shells or twists
185 g (6 oz) salami, diced

DRESSING:
6 tablespoons mayonnaise
2 eggs, hard-boiled and diced
2 tablespoons lime juice
2 teaspoons finely grated lime rind
4 tablespoons snipped chives
2 tablespoons chopped lemon thyme

TO GARNISH:
lemon thyme sprig

Cook the broad beans in boiling salted water for 5 minutes. Drain and set aside.

Cook the pasta until *al dente**. Drain and cool quickly under cold running water. Drain thoroughly and place in a large bowl. Stir in the beans and salami.

Mix the dressing ingredients together and fold into the pasta and beans. Spoon the salad into a serving bowl and garnish with a sprig of lemon thyme.

Serves 4 to 6

NOTE: If you are unable to obtain a lime, use lemon juice and rind instead, but use only 1 tablespoon lemon juice.

KOREAN NOODLES WITH NUTS

125 g (4 oz) snow peas
2 tablespoons oil
1 onion, sliced
1-2 cloves garlic, sliced
1-2 teaspoons each ground coriander and cumin
2 dried red chillies
315 g (10 oz) dried vermicelli
4 green shallots
125 g (4 oz) mushrooms
1 tablespoon chopped coriander
salt and pepper
1/4 cup pinenuts
1/4 cup flaked almonds, browned

DRESSING:
4 tablespoons olive oil
2 teaspoons soy sauce
1-2 tablespoons lime juice
1 teaspoon honey

TO GARNISH *(optional)*:
lime slices
coriander leaves

Cook the snow peas in boiling water for 1 minute, drain and set aside.

Heat the oil in a pan, add the onion and cook until golden. Add the garlic, coriander and cumin, then crumble in the chillies. Fry over a low heat for 2 minutes, stirring constantly. Remove from the heat and set aside.

Cook the vermicelli until *al dente**. Drain and cool quickly under cold running water. Drain thoroughly and place in a large bowl. Add the cooked spices and mix well.

Chop the green shallots and slice the mushrooms. Add to the vermicelli with the snow peas and coriander, and season with salt and pepper to taste.

Mix the dressing ingredients together, pour over the salad and mix well. Transfer to a serving dish and sprinkle with the nuts. Garnish with lime slices and coriander, if liked.

Serves 4 to 6

TAGLIATELLE SALAD

500 g (1 lb) fresh wholewheat tagliatelle
2 × 440 g cans red kidney beans
2 × 200 g cans tuna fish
4 young zucchini
60 g (2 oz) mushrooms
2 green shallots
1 tablespoon green peppercorns

DRESSING:
4 tablespoons mayonnaise
2 tablespoons each chopped parsley and chives
2 teaspoons lemon juice
1 teaspoon finely grated lemon rind
cayenne pepper
salt

TO GARNISH:
mint sprigs (optional)
lemon slices

Cook the tagliatelle until *al dente**. Drain and cool quickly under cold running water. Drain thoroughly and place in a large bowl.

Rinse and drain the kidney beans under cold running water. Drain and flake the tuna. Thinly slice the zucchini and mushrooms; chop the green shallots. Add to the pasta with the peppercorns.

Mix the dressing ingredients together, seasoning with cayenne pepper and salt to taste. Fold into the salad and transfer to a large serving bowl.

Garnish with mint sprigs if using, and lemon slices. Serve immediately.

Serves 4 to 6

PIZZA & PASTA PARTIES

A pizza or pasta party can be a great way to entertain. They are informal and simple to prepare, once you've mastered the basic doughs. These four menus each form a good basis for a party, but do give them your own personal touch by adding favourite ingredients to sauces and toppings.

If you wish to serve a starter, offer an hors d'oeuvre tray. Include a selection of meats and fish – such as salami, garlic sausage, Parma or smoked ham, tongue, sardines, anchovies and tuna fish – with vegetables like artichokes, onion rings, cauliflower florets, mushrooms, celery and peppers, as well as hard-boiled eggs, olives, melon and tomatoes. Arrange them in groups with suitable dressings and attractive garnishes.

If you wish to serve a simple dessert, a fruit salad is always popular. Serve the one on page 91, or make up your own.

Pizza Party for 10
Fennel and Orange Salad
Potato and Dill Salad
Party Pizza
Summer Pudding

Pizza Party for 20
Italian Rice Salad
Snow Pea Salad
Chilli Seafood Pizza
Blackcurrant Ice Cream
Lemon Tart

Pasta Party for 15
Greek Salad
Lasagne Verdi al Forno
Italian Fruit Salad

Pasta Party for 20
Broad Bean and Fennel Salad
Creamed Chicken with Noodles
Chocolate and Orange Mousse
Hazelnut and Raspberry Torte

GREEK SALAD

1 kg (2 lb) tomatoes
2 each red and yellow peppers, cored
1½ cucumbers, diced
3 onions, sliced
250 g (8 oz) black olives
375 g (12 oz) feta cheese, diced
2 tablespoons chopped parsley
DRESSING:
2 × 200 g cartons natural yogurt
2 teaspoons Dijon mustard
5 tablespoons lemon juice
2 tablespoons finely grated lemon rind
3 cloves garlic, crushed
small bunch chopped mint
salt and pepper

First make the dressing: put the yogurt, mustard, lemon juice and rind into a bowl and mix well. Stir in the garlic, mint, and salt and pepper to taste.

Thinly slice the tomatoes and peppers and arrange on a serving plate with the remaining salad ingredients. Spoon over the dressing and toss lightly to serve.

Serves 15

BROAD BEAN AND FENNEL SALAD

1.5 kg (3-3½ lb) shelled broad beans
salt and pepper
6 green shallots, chopped
4 heads of fennel, chopped
juice of 2 lemons
½ cup flaked almonds, toasted
DRESSING:
2-3 cloves garlic, crushed
pinch of cayenne pepper
2 × 200 g cartons natural yogurt
4 tablespoons chopped mint
grated rind of 2 limes

Cook the beans in boiling salted water for 5 minutes, until just tender. Drain and cool under cold running water. Drain thoroughly and place in a large bowl. Add the green shallots. Toss the fennel in the lemon juice and add both to the beans.

Mix the dressing ingredients together, adding salt and pepper to taste, spoon over the salad and toss well.

Pile into a serving dish, sprinkle with the almonds and garnish with mint and fennel leaves if liked.

Serves 20

POTATO AND DILL SALAD

1 kg (2 lb) new potatoes
salt and pepper
3 spring onions
7 tablespoons mayonnaise
good pinch of cayenne pepper
1 bunch of dill, roughly chopped
2 tablespoons sunflower seeds, toasted
dill sprigs to garnish

Cook the potatoes in boiling salted water for 15 minutes, until tender. Drain and cool, then slice them into a bowl.

Chop the spring onions into 2.5 cm (1 inch) pieces and add to the bowl with the mayonnaise and cayenne. Season with salt and pepper to taste. Stir in the dill.

Transfer to a serving dish and sprinkle with the sunflower seeds. Garnish with dill to serve.

Serves 10

ITALIAN RICE SALAD

500 g chicken soup bones
1 bouquet garni
1 large onion
3¾ cups Italian patna rice
⅔ cup dry white wine
salt and pepper
2 each red, green and yellow peppers, cored, seeded and chopped
250 g (8 oz) tomatoes, seeded and chopped
250 g (8 oz) Italian salami, diced
8 basil and 8 oregano sprigs, chopped
1 cup cashew nuts

DRESSING:

2 teaspoons Dijon mustard
6 tablespoons red wine vinegar
12 tablespoons olive oil
4 cloves garlic, crushed
3 teaspoons clear honey

Put the chicken bones in a large pan of cold water with the bouquet garni and onion. Bring to the boil, cover and simmer for 1 to 1½ hours. Strain, reserving the stock. Remove any meat from the bones, chop and set aside.

Place the rice, reserved stock, wine, and salt to taste in a large pan and cook for 12 to 15 minutes, until tender. Drain off any remaining liquid and cool.

Place the rice in a large bowl and stir in the chopped chicken meat.

Mix the dressing ingredients together, seasoning with salt and pepper to taste. Pour over the rice and mix well.

Fold in the remaining ingredients and transfer to a serving dish.

Serves 20

SNOW PEA SALAD

250 g (8 oz) streaky bacon, derinded
1 kg (2 lb) snow peas
salt and pepper
2 tablespoons each chopped thyme and parsley

DRESSING:

2 teaspoons peppercorn mustard
4 cloves garlic, crushed
2 teaspoons clear honey
4 tablespoons lime juice
8 tablespoons olive oil
3 tablespoons chopped parsley
2 tablespoons chopped thyme

Grill the bacon until crisp. Leave to cool, then crumble or chop and set aside.

Mix all the dressing ingredients together, seasoning with salt and pepper to taste.

Blanch the snow peas in boiling salted water for 2 minutes. Drain, cool under cold running water and drain thoroughly.

Toss the snow peas in the dressing, then mix in the bacon and chopped herbs. Transfer to a serving dish and garnish with lime slices and parsley if liked.

Serves 20

PARTY PIZZA

*1½ quantity pizza dough**
1½ quantity Tomato Sauce (see American Hot Pizza, page 30)
125 g (4 oz) button mushrooms, sliced
8 canned artichoke hearts, sliced
6 tomatoes, sliced
6 oregano sprigs
1 × 200 g can tuna fish, drained
2 tablespoons capers
2 × 45 g cans anchovies, drained
60 g (2 oz) green olives, chopped
125 g (4 oz) salami
60 g (2 oz) mozzarella cheese, diced
125 g (4 oz) ham
60 g (2 oz) sweetcorn
2 teaspoons dried mixed herbs
2 tablespoons olive oil
¾ cup grated matured cheddar cheese

Roll out the dough to fit a large baking sheet, measuring 25 × 30 cm (10 × 12 inches); turn during rolling to prevent shrinking.

Place on a large piece of floured cardboard. Using fingertips, push the dough out from the centre to make the edges twice as thick as the rest.

Spread with the tomato sauce. Using a palette knife, lightly divide the dough into 6 sections.

Arrange the mushrooms and artichokes in one section; the tomatoes and oregano in another; the flaked tuna and capers in the third; the mashed anchovies and olives in the fourth; the sliced salami and mozzarella cheese in the fifth; and the sliced ham and sweetcorn in the last section.

Sprinkle the whole pizza with the mixed herbs, oil and grated cheese.

Slide the pizza onto the hot baking sheet* and bake in a preheated very hot oven, 230°C (450°F), for 15 to 20 minutes. Cut into slices and serve immediately.

Serves 10

CHILLI SEAFOOD PIZZA

*3 × quantity pizza dough**
3 × quantity Tomato Sauce (see American Hot Pizza, page 30)
2 tablespoons dried oregano
8 green chilli peppers, seeded and thinly sliced
3 × 200 g cans tuna fish, drained and flaked
315 g (10 oz) peeled prawns
375 g (12 oz) Bel Paese cheese, grated
2 × 45 g cans anchovies, drained
125 g (4 oz) stuffed olives, halved

Roll out the dough to fit 3 large baking sheets, measuring 25 × 30 cm (10 × 12 inches). Turn the dough during rolling to prevent shrinking.

Place on 2 or 3 large pieces of floured cardboard. Using the fingertips, push the dough from the centre outwards to make the edges twice as thick as the rest.

Spread with the tomato sauce and sprinkle with the oregano. Spoon over the chillies, tuna and prawns, and sprinkle with the cheese. Arrange the anchovies in a lattice over the top and decorate with the olives.

Slide the pizza onto the hot baking sheets* and bake in a preheated very hot oven, 230°C (450°F), for 15 to 20 minutes. Serve immediately.

Serves 20

LASAGNE VERDI AL FORNO

8 tablespoons olive oil
3 onions, chopped
6 cloves garlic, crushed
4 celery sticks, chopped
1 kg (2 lb) minced beef
250 g (8 oz) chicken livers, chopped
salt and pepper
3¾ cups dry white wine
3 × 400 g cans tomatoes
1 teaspoon grated nutmeg
2 teaspoons dried mixed herbs
12 sheets dried lasagne verdi
1¼ cups Béchamel sauce (see Baked Rigatoni, page 53)
1 cup grated parmesan cheese
¼ cup grated matured cheddar cheese
2 tablespoons dried breadcrumbs

Heat the oil in a large pan, add the onions and 4 cloves garlic and cook for 10 minutes, until pale golden. Stir in the celery and cook for 2 minutes.

Increase the heat and add the minced beef. Cook rapidly until lightly browned. Add the chicken livers, and season liberally with salt and pepper.

Pour over the wine, add the tomatoes with their juice, nutmeg and herbs. Bring to the boil, cover and simmer very gently for 2½ to 3 hours, stirring occasionally; if the mixture becomes too thick, add a little more wine. Stir in the remaining garlic and check the seasoning.

Spoon enough sauce into a very large ovenproof dish or roasting pan to cover the base. Arrange some lasagne over this. Repeat the layers until all the sauce and lasagne are used, finishing with lasagne.

Spoon over the Béchamel sauce and sprinkle with the cheeses and breadcrumbs.

Bake in a preheated hot oven, 200°C (400°F), for 45 to 50 minutes, until golden. Serve immediately.

Serves 15

CREAMED CHICKEN WITH NOODLES

2 size 18 oven-ready chickens
3 large onions, halved
1 bottle dry white wine
1 large bouquet garni
salt and pepper
125 g (4 oz) butter
8 shallots, chopped
3-4 cloves garlic, crushed
1 kg (2 lb) tomatoes, skinned, seeded and chopped
2 tablespoons each chopped basil and parsley
3 tablespoons chopped thyme
2½ cups cream
2 kg (4 lb) fresh tagliatelle
125 g (4 oz) butter
fresh herbs to garnish

Place the chickens in a large roasting pan. Add the onions, wine, bouquet garni, and salt and pepper to taste. Cover with foil and cook in a preheated moderate oven, 180°C (350°F), for 2½ hours, until very tender; cool.

Remove the flesh from the chickens and cut into small pieces. Remove the fat from the top of the liquid and strain the stock.

Melt the butter in a large pan, add the shallots and garlic and cook gently for 10 minutes. Add the tomatoes and herbs, and season with salt and pepper. Stir in the strained stock.

Bring to the boil, cover and simmer for 40 minutes. Remove lid and cook rapidly until thickened. Stir in the cream and chicken; set aside.

Cook the tagliatelle in 2 large pans until *al dente**. Drain and return to the pans. Divide the butter between the pans and toss well.

Heat the sauce, without boiling, pour over the pasta and toss well.

Transfer to a warmed serving dish and garnish with herbs. Serve with grated parmesan cheese.

Serves 20

BLACKCURRANT ICE CREAM

1.5 kg (3 lb) fresh or frozen blackcurrants
2¼ cups caster sugar
3¾ cups water
grated rind and juice of 1 lemon
5½ cups cream, lightly whipped

Place the blackcurrants in a large pan, with the sugar, water, lemon rind and juice. Bring to the boil, cover and simmer for 12 to 15 minutes, until the fruit is soft.

Leave to cool, then place the fruit and syrup in a food processor or an electric blender and work until smooth. Rub through a nylon sieve to remove pips. Fold the fruit purée into the cream.

Spoon the mixture into a rigid freezerproof container and freeze until firm. Remove from the freezer and whisk well. Refreeze for 2 hours, then whisk again. Return the ice cream to the container, cover, seal and freeze until firm.

Transfer to the refrigerator 30 minutes before serving to soften. Spoon into chilled dishes to serve.
Serves 12 to 16

SUMMER PUDDING

1 kg (2 lb) mixed summer fruits, e.g. blackcurrants, raspberries, redcurrants
¾-1 cup sugar
12 trifle sponge cakes

Put the fruits in a large saucepan, cover and bring slowly to the boil. Simmer for 7 to 10 minutes. Remove from the heat, stir in the sugar to taste and leave to cool.

Slice the sponge cakes in half lengthwise and use to line the base and sides of a 6-cup pudding basin. Spoon in three quarters of the stewed fruit and top with the remaining sponge cakes. Spoon over a little more fruit. Cover with a saucer or plate, gently pushing down. Leave in the refrigerator overnight.

Remove the plate, run a palette knife around the edge of the pudding and turn out onto a deep serving plate. Spoon over the remaining fruit and serve with whipped cream.
Serves 10

LEMON TART

PASTRY:
1½ cups plain flour
2 tablespoons caster sugar
125 g (4 oz) cold butter, cut into small pieces
1 egg yolk
FILLING:
¾ cup sugar
⅔ cup fresh lemon juice
½ cup orange juice
grated rind of 3 lemons
4 eggs
60 g (2 oz) butter
4 tablespoons cream
TO FINISH:
2 lemons, cut into segments
icing sugar, sifted

Sift the flour onto a pastry board and stir in the sugar. Make a hollow in the centre and add the butter and egg yolk. Using the fingertips, lightly bring the flour mixture into the centre over the butter and egg to combine the ingredients. Knead lightly and form into a ball. Dust with flour, cover with plastic wrap and chill for 1 hour.

Roll out the dough and use to line a 25 cm (10 inch) flan tin with removable base. Prick with a fork and chill for 1 hour. Line the pastry case with greaseproof paper and dried beans and bake in a preheated hot oven, 200°C (400°F), for 10 to 15 minutes, until lightly browned. Remove the greaseproof paper and baking beans.

Place the sugar, lemon and orange juice, rind and eggs in a bowl and beat together. Melt the butter in a pan, stir in the cream, add the egg mixture and cook over a low heat, stirring, until thickened; take care not to scramble the eggs and do not boil. Remove from the heat, transfer to a bowl and cover the surface with dampened greaseproof paper. Cover the bowl with plastic wrap and leave to cool.

Spoon the custard into the pastry case and bake in a preheated moderately hot oven, 190°C (375°F), for 20 minutes.

Arrange the lemon segments on top and sprinkle liberally with icing sugar. Place under a preheated hot grill for 1 minute until golden brown. Serve warm or cold with cream.

Serves 10 to 12

NOTE: If you think most of your guests will want a portion of each dessert make two of these tarts.

ITALIAN FRUIT SALAD

2½ cups orange juice
grated rind of 2 lemons
6 tablespoons lemon juice
125 g (4 oz) black cherries
½ rock melon
3 bananas
4 nectarines
1 mango
3 peaches
3 apricots
4 green eating apples
2 pears
125 g (4 oz) white seedless grapes (optiona)
about ¼ cup caster sugar
10 tablespoons Maraschino liqueur

Put the orange juice, lemon rind and juice in a large bowl.

Prepare the fruit, adding to the bowl as you do so: stone the cherries, scoop the melon into small balls using a melon baller; slice the bananas; stone and slice the nectarines, mango, peaches and apricots; core and slice the apples and pears. Add the grapes and stir well.

Sprinkle over the sugar to taste and the Maraschino and stir well. Cover and chill for 1 hour.

Serve with cream and crisp biscuits.

Serves 15

NOTE: Use this recipe as a guide, using fruits in season.

CHOCOLATE AND ORANGE MOUSSE

375 g (12 oz) dark chocolate
45 g (1½ oz) butter
6 eggs, separated
grated rind and juice of 2 oranges
2 tablespoons brandy
TO DECORATE:
⅔ cup cream, whipped
2 chocolate flakes, broken into pieces

Break the chocolate into a heatproof bowl over a pan of hot water. Stir occasionally until melted, then stir in the butter and blend well. Add the egg yolks and mix well. Remove from the heat. Stir in the orange rind and juice and the brandy.

Whisk the egg whites until very stiff and fold into the chocolate mixture. Transfer to a serving dish and chill for 3 hours.

Decorate with whipped cream and chocolate flake to serve.

Serves 10 to 12

HAZELNUT AND RASPBERRY TORTE

250 g (8 oz) hazelnuts
1¼ cups plain flour
salt
¾ cup icing sugar, sifted
125 g (4 oz) unsalted butter, softened
1 egg yolk
FILLING:
1¼ cups cream, whipped
¼ cup cranberry sauce
250 g (8 oz) fresh raspberries
TO DECORATE:
½ cup cream, whipped
whole raspberries
hazelnuts, toasted

Place the hazelnuts under a hot grill for a few minutes to brown. Remove the skins and grind coarsely.

Sift the flour and a pinch of salt on to a board. Make a well in the centre, put in the hazelnuts, icing sugar, butter and egg yolk. Work the flour into the centre, using the fingertips, and mix to a smooth paste. Cover and chill for 1 hour.

Divide the dough into 4. Roll out each piece into a 20 cm (8 inch) circle and place on lightly greased baking sheets. Prick each circle with a fork and chill for 1 hour.

Bake in a preheated moderately hot oven, 190°C (375°F) for 8 to 10 minutes, until golden. Cool on wire racks.

Place one round on a serving plate. Mix together the whipped cream and cranberry sauce and use a third to cover the biscuit base. Cover with a third of the raspberries and place another biscuit round on top. Repeat the layers twice more, finishing with a biscuit round.

Spread half the whipped cream in a thin layer over the top of the torte; use the remaining cream to pipe rosettes around the edge. Finish with raspberries and hazelnuts.

Serves 12

NOTE: If you think all of your guests will choose the torte, double the quantities and make two!

INDEX

ACKNOWLEDGMENTS
Recipes devised and food prepared by Caroline Ellwood
Photography by Charlie Stebbings
Photographic stylist: Liz Hippisley